NATURAL
MEDITATION

NATURAL MEDITATION

REFRESHING YOUR SPIRIT THROUGH NATURE

BARBARA ANN KIPFER

Skyhorse Publishing

To Paul, Kyle, Keir, and Hoops

A NOTE FROM THE AUTHOR

Natural Meditation offers meditations carried out in nature or while visualizing nature. There are easy-to-follow entries about meditating in natural settings or meditating on natural scenes or objects. The book also has sidebars with thoughts about incorporating nature in one's mindfulness practice. Readers can open to a page during lunch break, at home in the evening, or on the weekend and take a short "retreat," setting off down a quiet, natural path.

This book acknowledges that nature has a lot to teach us about going with the flow, letting go, awareness, calm, silence, pausing, and non-materialism. Whether readers do these meditations in actual natural settings or on a cushion at home, the book's entries will inspire readers to spend more time in nature.

Natural Meditation emphasizes the spiritual, moral, and other tangible benefits of nature. The focus is on training the mind in relaxation, visualization, creativity, and rejuvenation—incorporating natural settings, plants, and animals. Sometimes a respite or quiet path is just what one needs in this crazy world, a few minutes to take time to slow down, breathe, be awake and aware, and appreciate.

Barbara Ann Kipfer

Sometimes you are outside, say at the beach, and noises created by other people "ruin" your time there. This, of course, also happens inside in various situations, but when you are in nature, you may have expectations of peace and quiet. When others produce unexpected and unwanted noise, you are very much challenged. Here is a practice that will come in handy both outside and inside. Go to a place in nature that is frequented by a lot of people, like the beach. Walk for a bit, using all of your senses to absorb the sights, smells, and sounds of nature in that place. Then find a place to meditate, sitting or lying down, eyes closed or open—whatever is comfortable physically, but also within earshot of people who are making noise that you find disturbing. When negative emotions start to come up due to unwanted noise, be present with them, labeling the feeling, noting any place in the body where you feel them strongest, and breathe in and out with your mental and physical reactions. By watching your feelings, labeling them, and not adding in thoughts, you will find that your emotions may start to ebb. But the thoughts might just barge right in along with your judgments about the people making noise. Observe the feelings of separateness and upset you feel, with both the people and the place itself, then return to focusing on your breath and bodily sensations. Over time, being mindful of your reactions will help you find ways to create a spaciousness to help you overcome your fixation on the unwanted noise and, instead, refocus on the pleasant aspects of the natural scene.

Stop and smell the flowers.

As you walk, bicycle, run, or just sit on the porch, notice the natural objects and weather around you. Look carefully at the overall landscape of the area. As you walk, you may see, hear, or smell something that you want to savor. Enjoy what you encounter and breathe to be fully present.

Imagine a world without birds, how lifeless it would seem. Birds rule their own element, delighting us with their beauty, in particular, of plumage and song. They are the natural analogue of angels, and symbolize the links between heaven and earth. When you think of the soul's ecstasy or transcendence, flight is the image many of us seize upon. Spend time watching birds, through binoculars or with the naked eye, and listen to their glorious songs in the season of courtship. No creatures stir the heart to greater enjoyment. Bird watching, far from being a sublimated form of hunting, offers a true appreciation of wonderful moments in nature. Look out for homecoming migrants. Celebrate, for example, your first swallow of the summer, rejoicing in its amazing double feat of long-distance flight and accurate navigation.

Rake leaves and jump in the pile.

Go out into your favorite place in nature, a place where you can feel relaxed. Lie on your back on a mat, pad, or towel with your legs uncrossed, your arms at your sides, palms up, and your eyes open or closed in relaxation pose. Focus on your breathing, how the air moves in and out of your body. Slowly and deeply breathe in through your nose and out through your mouth or nose. After several slow, deep breaths, as you begin to feel comfortable and relaxed, direct your attention to the toes of your left foot. Tune into any sensations in that part of your body while remaining aware of your breathing. It often helps to imagine each breath flowing to the spot where you are directing your attention. Focus on your left toes for one to two minutes. Then move your focus to the sole of your left foot and hold it there for a minute or two while continuing to pay attention to your breathing. Follow the same procedure as you move to your left ankle, calf, knee, thigh, hip, and so on all around the body. Then move to the right side of your body beginning, again, with your right toes, and continue until you have gone all around the body. Pay particular attention to the head: the jaw, chin, lips, tongue, roof of the mouth, nostrils, throat, cheeks, eyelids, eyes, eyebrows, forehead, temples, and scalp. Finally, focus on the very top of your hair, the uppermost part of your body.

Watching is meditation. What you watch is irrelevant. You can watch the trees, the river, clouds, children playing. The quality of observation, the quality of being aware and alert, that is what meditation is. Meditation means awareness. Anything having to do with awareness is meditation.

In the twelfth century, Zen-minded spiritual seekers used the ten Ox-Herding Pictures to help them find enlightenment. The ox is a symbol of our true nature. The Ox-Herding Pictures show the following: A man is looking for his ox, he finds footprints, he glimpses the ox, then manages (just) to hang on to it, then tames it and rides it home happily. In the seventh picture there's no ox, only the man. In the eighth image, an empty circle—the man has vanished, too. In the ninth, there is pure landscape. In the tenth, the man, barefoot, enters the marketplace with giving hands. Inner wisdom enables us to forget the self, see the world as it is, and reenter the community of souls to participate helpfully in its joys and sorrows. Ponder the sequence, and follow it in your life.

Let nature enhance your meditation.

Leaves on a stream exercise: Sit in a comfortable position by a body of water, if possible. This is a visualization exercise, but the sound of flowing water makes it feel even more real. So, close your eyes and visualize a gently flowing stream with leaves floating along the surface of the water. For the next few minutes, take each thought that enters your mind and place it on a leaf. Let each leaf float by. Do this with each thought—pleasurable, painful, or neutral. Even if you have a joyous or enthusiastic thought, place them on a leaf and let them float by. If your thoughts momentarily stop, continue to watch the stream. Sooner or later, your thoughts will start up again. Allow the stream to flow at its own pace. You are not trying to rush the leaves along or get rid of your thoughts. You are allowing them to come and go at their own pace. If a leaf gets stuck, allow it to hang around until it is ready to float by. If a difficult or painful feeling arises, simply acknowledge it. Say to yourself, *I notice boredom/impatience/frustration.* Place those thoughts on leaves and allow them to float along. As soon as you realize that you have become hooked on one thought, gently bring your attention back to the visualization exercise.

Take a walk, paying close attention to all of nature, but with a different attitude. Look at everything as though you have never seen it before. Pick things up, smell them, feel them. Become a child again in a world of discovery. With each step, try counting three new things you see.

A tidepool is a miniature world often teeming with life, and all the more precious for being temporary. At the seaside, recapture the joys of childhood by finding a weedy tidepool and crouching down to observe its inhabitants going about their business. The middle reaches of the shore have the liveliest pools, with sponges, anemones, worms, snails, crabs, other crustaceans, and even fishes. These creatures live right at the fringes of our everyday concerns: to visit from time to time refreshes our enthusiasm and wonder. As you walk along the shore, reflect on human origins: land animals like ourselves developed from amphibious creatures that evolved in the tidal zone, so without the tides, and therefore without the moon, there would have been no people.

Look for the rainbow when it rains.

Hike through a city, state, or national park for meditation. Hiking in nature provides an opportunity to tune in, both to your own experience and to the world around you. While it can be easy to get lost in thoughts or daydreams while hiking, the simple practices of mindfulness can draw you more closely into your experience of the natural world. Start by paying attention to each step. Simply notice each time your foot makes contact with the ground. Notice your body, moving through space. Feel the contact of air against your skin. Bring your awareness to your senses: touch, smell, sight, hearing. What do you feel, smell, notice, hear? Allow each sensation to wash over you, not holding on to any one, but gently receiving each as you notice it. When hiking uphill, take your time. Let your weight come fully into each step before you take the next one, and find a pace that allows your breathing to have a steady rhythm. Find moments to stop and receive the experience: at the top of a hill, looking over a view, at a junction in the trail, or in front of a beautiful flower or tree. Feel your feet on the ground, your body in space, and notice the movement of the environment around you.

Imagine a pool deep in the earth that is a source of vitality and energy. Breathing in, you feel the liquid light rise like a fountain into your feet, up the legs, into the spine, and to the top of your head. Breathing out, the energy cascades back to the ground and you feel cleansed.

In Celtic symbolism, the birch tree represents new beginnings. Babies' cradles were made of birch wood, and bundles of birch were used to sweep the house at the Celtic new year. Birch also has strong fertility connections: The tree was often used as a maypole, and, according to Scottish folklore, a cow herded with a birch stick would give birth to a healthy calf. When you next encounter a creative block, go sit under a birch tree. Touch its trunk, pick up a fallen leaf. Or just look at a picture of a birch in a book. Tune into the tree's ancient symbolism and allow it to cleanse you of the old, and inspire you with the new.

Seek beauty in art, music, and nature.

One of the best ways to calm and quiet your mind is to cultivate bare attention, the ability to be awake and aware of the present moment without "adding on" to the moment with thoughts or mental commentary. So, here is a meditation practice for being in nature without clinging to thoughts, commentary, or judgment. Go outside and choose a natural object that attracts you. Looking at it, try to let go of any previous associations or memories involved with the object. Simply experience everything you can about the object as it is through your senses of touch, smell, hearing, and sight. Try to keep going deeper into your "knowing" of the object. When you start narrating in your mind, acknowledge what is happening and let go of the thoughts. You will be able to take what you learn from this practice and use it in other areas of your life: in time spent with family and friends, and during times when you are at work, shopping, or other experiences. Think about the difference between bare attention and the experiences in which you are listening to your thoughts instead of being in the moment.

If you feel attuned to a certain type of animal, you may want to create an animal altar. You could have an image or statue of the animal as well as objects from nature such as fresh flowers that the animal is connected with. Each day you can meditate there or offer a prayer for the animal.

Metaphors and similes are the most instantaneous way available to us for creating an imaginative effect. It's no accident that this is a frequent device in poetry. However, it's also a highly creative way of looking at the world in general; it can enrich your perceptions and your conversation. Look out for similarities and express them to yourself or others. You might imagine that a thought is like a cloud, or a smile is like a promise, or a kiss is like a butterfly, landing on your lips and then taking off again. Make metaphor an essential part of your perceptions.

There are many things in nature that we are uncomfortable with, such as bugs and nasty weather. There are unpleasant things that you cannot control, just like inside. Perhaps you are trying to sit outside in the sun and you get bitten by a horsefly. You are at a pumpkin patch in the fall and yellow jackets are preventing you from enjoying your picnic. You want to walk around the city to look at the Christmas decorations, but the biting wind is taking all the fun out of it. It's good to examine your reactions to these types of outdoor irritations. If you can observe how you feel during these times, you begin to sense the impermanence involved in the annoyances and irritations. And you can practice letting go of your feelings of hatred, dislike, or upset, being in the moment just as it is. This is a very difficult but worthwhile practice to explore. When you can recognize that what is happening is not personal, is going to change, and that your expectations are factoring into your suffering, you can learn a valuable lesson that will be one of the most important you can absorb.

Meditate on a wooden table's history. Imagine it as a tiny seed, then as a young sapling, then a mature, stoic tree. See its felling, its processing. Imagine a carpenter constructing the table with tender loving care. Give thanks to the wooden table now that it serves a purpose for you.

For centuries the gods were thought to be cloud-dwellers, and heaven itself has been located in the sky. But to imagine spirituality as ethereal and remote is fundamentally mistaken. Your spirit combines all four elements. It has the fire of passion, and the purifying flames that burn off unwanted trappings of the ego. It has the fluidity of water, molding itself to circumstances. Like air, it is weightless, in the sense of being free of heavy burdens. And, lastly, it keeps its feet firmly on the ground. Earth is one of spirit's elements, not its opposite.

Go to a local park and swing on the swings.

If you are mindful as you shovel snow, the experience can improve our health, safety, and overall well-being. Pay attention to the feeling of your boots walking on the snow. Be aware of any ice that may cause you to slip. Pay attention to the snowfall. Newly fallen snow is lighter than heavily packed or partially melted snow. Notice your body. Are you cold? Pick up the shovel. Space your hands out. As you prepare to lift the snow, stand with your feet about shoulder-width apart to maintain balance. Bend at the knees, not the waist or back. Lift with your legs. Notice the tightening of your stomach muscles as you lift. Exhale as you lift. Keep the shovel close to your body. Take your time. Pace yourself. Enjoy the quiet moment and continue removing the snow, one shovelful at a time. Focus your attention on your breath as it flows in and out of your body. Stay in touch with the different sensations of each inhale and exhale without looking for anything special to happen. No need to alter or change your breathing, just observe.

Try taking impeccable care of something in nature for a week: a pet, a plant, a tree, your lawn. At the end of the week, notice if you feel closer to what you took care of. Making the connection that caring *for* something leads to caring *about* something can be an important insight on the spiritual path.

Snow can disrupt, damage, and annoy, but in temperate regions it's often a benign spectral visitor, transforming familiar landscapes. If you can, get out among it: go sledding, even if snow is still falling. As the old saying puts it, bad weather always looks worse through a window. After a good snowfall, it's fun to recapture childhood by tobogganing, throwing snowballs, or lying down on your back in the snow and waving your arms across the surface to make a snow angel—a wonderfully pointless gesture, expressing sheer joy in the moment.

Save the lives of animals about to be killed.

Pausing or stopping is a great practice anywhere, but it is most effective when done in nature. So, whether you are biking, hiking, walking, playing tennis, picnicking, or lying on a beach, all you have to do is regularly stop what you are doing and pay attention to what each of your senses takes in. When you stop what you're doing in the moment and close your eyes for a few minutes, attend to what you hear without naming what it is—a pure sensing of the sound. Notice where you feel the sounds in your ear and any part of your body where there is a vibration. And note the silences, too. Then move on to hearing, smelling, and finally, seeing. The last one is done with eyes open and it is the most challenging to keep simple, to focus on the experience while letting go of any related thoughts or urge to describe the experience in words. At the end of this practice, note what effects that stopping to be completely with the sensations had on your mind, body, and spirit. Reenter your activity with the heightened awareness you gained.

See yourself in a beautiful courtyard filled with exotic flowers. In the center is a fountain of crystal-clear water and there are drinking cups. Step forward, choose a cup, and fill it from the fountain. Let this drink fill your mind, body, and spirit with new life and vitality.

A life filled with complex flow activities like hiking or long walks is more worth living than one spent consuming passive entertainment. Breathing exercises help you cultivate the conscious intention to transcend yourself and to enter into the flow of consciousness. If you are interested in something, you will focus on it, and if you focus your attention on anything, it is likely that you will become interested in it. Many of the things you find interesting are not so by nature, but are so because you took the trouble of paying attention to them.

Find a quiet place outdoors and sit on a cushion, pillow, pad, towel, mat, rolled-up piece of clothing, a log, or a smooth rock. Let your eyes close gently. Invite your body to relax and release into the ground or cushion. Let go and accept non-doing. Become sensitive to and listen to your breath. Breathe through your nose. Feel the air as it goes in and out. Feel the rising and falling of the chest and abdomen. Allow your attention to settle where you feel the breath most clearly. Follow the breath. Allow the breath to be as it is without controlling it. See the space or pause between breaths. Thinking will start. It is a habit. See each thought like a railroad car of a train going by. See it, acknowledge it, let it go, and come back to the breath. It does not matter how many times you get caught up in a thought or for how long. Begin again and bring awareness back to the breath. You are strengthening mindfulness. Awareness of one whole in-breath and one whole out-breath is a big accomplishment.

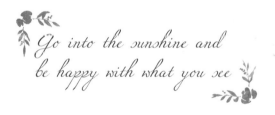

Go into the sunshine and be happy with what you see

Spend a walk focusing on the shadows created by natural objects. This way of seeing the shadow world cultivates awareness and perception beyond the normal. It helps you perceive the background of your everyday world, when previously you focused on the foreground.

Green represents the qualities of abundance, growth, tranquility, and harmony in cultures from Celtic to Chinese. Spend as much time as you can in green spaces and notice their soothing, even healing effect. Bring nature to you by introducing plants into your home, or carrying a green-tinted crystal. Green aventurine is especially powerful: it calms the emotions, encourages a positive outlook, and promotes spiritual growth.

Silent meditation: For three to five minutes, conceive of the Mind of the Universe, the Mind that manages all things. Then for three to five minutes, conceive of the Intelligence of the Universe, which produces all things. Then visualize the two joining within you. Discover that while Mind and Intelligence are distinct from each other, they are One. Let the images flow together, like two streams converging into a river. Let this power fill your body. Open your eyes and break the silence by saying, "The Power is divided above and below." The One generates itself, makes itself grow, seeks itself, finds itself. Look for this power in your daily life.

Do a water-gazing meditation in the fall. Sit by the water. Count your breaths as if they are waves. Let the regular wavelike motion of the breath wash away your cares. Let it carry you home. Float on the breath of the present moment. Let the water meditate for you. Flow with it.

A snowflake is as precious as a diamond. Its characteristic shape is created by the hexagonal lattice of an ice crystal, branching out into tree-like patterns as it grows unevenly but symmetrically in midair. Each flake consists of billions of water molecules captured from the atmosphere, and some of these will inevitably be from our own exhalations. In a snow shower, let the flakes settle on your coat, and watch their precarious elegance dissolve like the thoughts of the ego fading.

Standing golden flower meditation: Stand and allow any tension to drop away from you. Breathe naturally. Imagine your spine is a straight stem. Feel it growing upward from your lower back. It continues up above your head until a large golden flower blooms. The flower head travels upward a little farther, pulling your spine straighter. At the same time, imagine your feet as the flower's roots. Feel your feet go deeper into the earth. Between the flower above your head and the roots that are your feet, feel your spine stretch out just a little more. Your arms and hands become the leaves, light as air. Now imagine energy, in the form of golden-white light, traveling up from the roots that are your feet, up through your spine to the top of your head, where the golden flower blooms. The light fills the flower with cleansing energy and revitalization. Hold this image. Then let the light descend your body, into the earth.

To feel rooted to the earth, first stand with all your weight on the right foot. Then stand with all your weight on the left foot. Do this four or five times. Feel the shift of energy. Then try to be just in the middle. That middle feeling gives you more rootedness to the earth.

We always feel fortunate when we see a rainbow, partly on account of its majesty, partly because it tells of sunshine after rain. It's also a heartening symbol of destiny, the belief that there's a path, even if we cannot know what lies at the end of it. Sometimes you might be lucky enough to see a double rainbow: one arc inside another, with the colors arranged in reverse order. Think of any rainbow as a blessing, the laws of physics translated into a moment of transcendent beauty we can all understand and rejoice in.

Let your mind become clear, like a still pond.

Try a visualization for healing. Check over your body and release any tension you are holding. When you are relaxed, begin the healing process. Imagine you are standing under a shower of whitish-blue light. The light comes in through the top of your head and washes through your body, clearing the body of impurities and toxins. Feel the light taking the impurities and toxins out of each part of your body, one by one. If any part of your body needs special healing, focus on that part and let the light purify it. When you feel cleansed, let those impurities flow out through the soles of your feet into the earth. Let the light flow back up through your body, filling it with healing energy. Hold an image of your whole body flooded with the healing light and then let the light ascend up through the top of your head and out into the universe. Take some deep breaths and close the meditation.

Tranquility is fostered by time alone and time in nature.

Call to mind the person or people or animals you love most. Visualize them and allow your feelings of love to rise up. Imagine you are embracing them and protecting them with this love. After you have done this, you can widen the circle of love to close friends and other people.

According to Tantric philosophy, contemplation of the lotus flower aids spiritual growth. Visualize yourself as a beautiful lotus flower, emerging from the mud of materialism through the waters of experience toward the sunshine of enlightenment, where you blossom. Just as the lotus stands in the mud and the water but has its own transcendent substance, so the events and circumstances of your life surround you but are not part of your unique essence—you need not identify yourself with them. Grow always toward the light.

Arriving at the beach, try to open up all of your senses: hearing, seeing, smelling, taste, and touch. See if you can stay present without getting lost in thoughts or judgments. Try lying down on the sand and letting your body relax. Feel the supportive quality of the earth as your body settles into the ground. Allow your muscles to release any tension as you let go of thoughts and simply come into the physical present. Then sit next to the water's edge. Close your eyes and listen to the sound of the waves crashing on the shore. Let your attention expand to the farthest thing you can hear. Then take a mindful walk along the water's edge. Feel the textures of the sand, and each time you inhale, smell the salty, fragrant air. Gaze at the horizon and take in the vastness of the seascape. Look at the clouds, the expanse of water, and the space all around you.

See yourself walking into a spiral maze of massive stones. With each step, you feel lighter and more connected to the spirit. By the time you reach the center, you are in touch with your intuition. Remain silent in the knowledge that the wisdom you need lies deep inside of you.

In the Native American tradition, each person has an animal spirit or totem that serves as an ally and protector. Is there an animal you feel drawn to, one that appears frequently in your dreams? If so, consider its main qualities. For example, cats are linked with mystery and independence; dogs with loyalty; cranes with longevity and solitude; deer with gentleness. Be aware of your animal spirit's presence within, and visualize its protective companionship guiding you whenever you feel lonely or worried.

Calmly light a soy or honey candle and brighten the earth.

Look at the food on the plate in front of you. Think about all the people who were involved in providing your breakfast, people who grew it or manufactured it or packaged it or delivered it, and the environment that sustained it. The fact that the food is in front of you is the sum of all the conditions that created that food. Likewise, the fact that you are where you are at this moment is a result of all the conditions that created you and sustained you and allowed you to be exactly where you are now. There are moments when it becomes absolutely clear that the entire history of the earth and the cosmos needed to be exactly the way it was in order for you to be exactly where you are now, eating your breakfast. Try to eat in a relaxed way, listening to the sounds around you, enjoying your food, enjoying being right where you are at this moment.

Walk with fresh eyes. Let a walk be an unfolding surprise.

Saying grace can provide a wonderful moment of thankful meditation before a meal. It need not be religious: simply giving thanks to the animals and plants who have given up their lives to make the meal, and to friends and family for coming together at the table, can be enough.

Let your imagination work with no expectations, exercising and nourishing it. Frank Lloyd Wright wrote, "An idea is salvation by imagination," and Henry David Thoreau said, "The world is but a canvas to imagination." Consider a tropical fish in an aquarium: he believes that the ocean is a ten-second swim from one glassy rock-face to another. We are all conditioned by our circumstances to believe that our lives are typical. Let your imagination rove, and find new possibilities for yourself.

T'an t'ien meditation: Begin by sitting with closed eyes and take a few deep breaths. Focus on your lower abdomen, at a point about two inches below your navel and about one inch inside your body. This is *t'an t'ien*, a focal point of chi. Direct your breath to this area, expanding it on the inhale and contracting it on the exhale. Breathe into the *t'an t'ien* for at least five minutes. Then start to imagine that you are a tree with roots that go deep into the earth. Visualize these roots originating in the *t'an t'ien* and going through the base of the spine into the ground, far down into the soil. Also visualize these roots drawing energy up from the earth into your *t'an t'ien* on inhalation. Feel energy spreading down through the roots on exhalation. You can end this meditation when your *t'an t'ien* feels charged and strong.

Even non-sounds make great reminders. Turning a light on or off, traffic lights, a smile, the sight of a flower, your cup of coffee ready to drink. Each of these can be used as a mindfulness bell to stop, breathe consciously, let go, then open your eyes to the present moment.

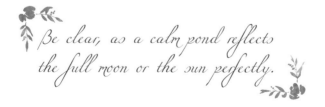

Be clear, as a calm pond reflects the full moon or the sun perfectly.

The moon offers an appealing focus for a visual meditation if you can contrive to obtain a decent view. Before you begin, think about the moon's coolness and serenity. While meditating, allow your mind to be filled with the image of the moon and an appreciation of its qualities. Any clouds drifting over the satellite add an atmospheric bonus. The moon is a messenger warning that your life is passing. The nature of all things and all appearances is like the reflection of the moon on water.

There are some fears involved with the great outdoors. You might be a new hiker and worry about what you will encounter, about getting lost, and about getting hurt. Perhaps you feel unsafe camping out in the dark. Meditation may help you to deal with fearful thoughts and emotions involved with unfamiliar situations outdoors. You can create some practice situations where you test entering into the environment for a short while, sitting and pondering your thoughts and fears. When these occur, you can sense the support of the earth, knowing that things will pass and change, and keep returning to your breath. You can choose a reassuring practice, like a loving-kindness (metta) meditation or a visualization, anything that helps relieve the fear bit by bit, knowing that overcoming fear takes time.

Commune with and learn from nature. Communicate with animals.

Pick an object that is thirty to sixty feet in front of you, like a certain part of a tree. Soften your gaze and notice what you can see peripherally at the edges of your vision. Do this, too, as you are walking or hiking, consciously tuning into and enjoying your peripheral vision.

The blessings that come from cultivating loving-kindness are: Your dreams become sweet. You fall asleep easily. You wake contented. Your thoughts are pleasant. Your health improves. Angels and devas will love and protect you. Animals will sense your love and not harm you. People will welcome you everywhere. Your babies will be happy. If you lose things, they will be returned. If you fall off a cliff, a tree will be there to catch you. The world will be more peaceful around you.

A meditation for cat people: Feel the way your cat settles into your lap. Notice the contours of the cat's body, its soft belly and its bony legs. Is the warmth all over your lap or is there a concentration, a warmest spot? Pet your cat from the head toward the tail, observing how the cat responds and reacts. Scratch your cat gently, starting at the top of the head and going down toward the jaw. Notice the change in the feeling of the fur, as it gets a little softer at the jawline. Listen to the purr and feel its vibrations in your lap. Look at your cat's eyes. Are they half-closed? Fully closed? Feel the cat's breath, and deepen your own inhalations and exhalations. When your cat gets up to leave, celebrate the feline declaration of independence and freely let them go.

When bending over to touch your toes, bow humbly to the earth.

Visualize walking into a spiral maze of massive stones. With each step, you feel lighter and more connected to the spirit. By the time you reach the center, you are in touch with your intuition. Remain silent in the knowledge that the wisdom you need lies deep inside of you.

The oak tree traditionally symbolizes wisdom, strength, and courage. It was regarded by Socrates as an oracle tree, and the Druids ate acorns in preparation for prophesying. When you next pass an old oak tree, take a moment to consider it in this light. Touch its mighty trunk, or sit under its graceful branches, and absorb its sense of history and wisdom. A little time tapping into its energy in this way may well help you to develop a clearer, braver vision of your own future.

Hug a tree. Reflect on its singularity and uniqueness and examine one leaf or some other small part of the tree. Recognize that despite that leaf's individuality and the stand-alone tree, both are interconnected to a much larger system and community. The leaf is connected to every other leaf and part of the tree, but also to the ground below, the sky above, the rain, the sun, and the ecosystem created by the other trees, plants, animals—and even humans. You have acknowledged the leaf and all that is contained in it, but you also see it is part of the web of life, an infinite, expansive universe. You learn about yourself through this exercise, that despite your differences from others, you are united with every living being.

The next time you feel yourself going into a downward spiral, turn inward. Instead of distracting yourself with something, sit down and breathe. Meditate and let things be. Meditation allows you to ride out the storms gracefully and detach from your personal ups and downs.

When you are experiencing difficult emotions, you may benefit greatly from meditating in nature. You can walk or sit in a place outside where you feel safe and can drink in the pleasantness and peacefulness of nature just being itself. Absorbing yourself in the sitting or walking and focusing on the nature around you will let some of the stress and pain drop away. You will feel connected to nature and more peaceful because of the quiet and calm aspects you will be drawn to.

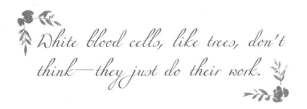

White blood cells, like trees, don't think—they just do their work.

Before you go outside to walk or do other exercise, sit and breathe until you are calm. If you are right-handed, concentrate on the left side of your body, particularly your left hand and foot. Visualize yourself walking toward a door. Imagine reaching out with your left hand and turning the handle. (Do the opposite if you are left-handed.) In your mind, begin to walk through the doorway, being mindful of taking the first step with your left foot. As you pass through the doorway, turn toward the left and close the door with your left hand. Once you have finished the visualization, imagine powerful energy coursing up your left side. Try to bring this increased awareness of your left side into your life after the meditation.

Meditate with the sounds of the outdoors. It could be the lovely sound of wind or rain, but could also be a revving motorcycle or a bird with an annoying and repetitive call. Be open and connect to the sounds. You will realize that the world is 99 percent out of your control.

In the narrow and crowded streets of a town in north India, an elephant was blocking the way to market. No one knew how to get by the beast. Then the townspeople saw a holy man walking down the street. If anyone knows what to do, he will, they said to each other. When they looked again, the guru had vanished. A few minutes later, when they looked toward the elephant, they saw him beyond the elephant, approaching the market stalls. He had simply made a detour around the block.

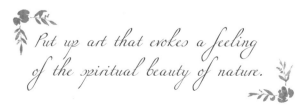

Put up art that evokes a feeling of the spiritual beauty of nature.

Consider doing labyrinth walking and seek cathedrals and other churches that have them. Or you can purchase canvas labyrinth walks for your backyard, smaller finger labyrinths for your home or desk, or you can mow a labyrinth in your back yard or a field by carving a simplified walkway out of the grass, or outlining a path with stones. Many people who make their own labyrinths find the act of creating a path to walk a wonderful part of the whole experience. The walk to the labyrinth's center has its twists and turns, even moments that feel like failure, for the path sometimes seems to be taking you in the opposite direction of where you feel you ought to go. Your negative thoughts drop away as you walk and focus inward.

If you keep a green bough in your heart, the singing bird will come.

Arrange your grocery cart as if it were a Zen rock garden. Mindfully place each chosen item into the cart to imitate the essence of nature. At the checkout counter, mindfully take each item out of the cart and place it on the conveyor. Bag your own groceries, mindfully.

The Maya were the first people to cultivate cocoa. It was so important to them that they traded it for other commodities, offered it at festivals in honor of their merchant god Ek Chuah, and gave the beans as precious gifts on occasions such as a child's coming of age. Next time you receive a box of chocolates as a gift, think back to this age when cocoa was so very valuable. Take a moment to appreciate what an amazing natural treasure your simple gift really is.

Take a walk outside and use the time to focus on desires and wants that arise in your mind. You might start thinking about the shower or cup of coffee that you want to enjoy upon your return. You might start wishing to get your work done quickly so you can do something more fun once it is wrapped up. Being in nature while paying attention to these thoughts makes them stand out and their influence becomes clearer. Natural settings are simple places filled with life and none of the things in nature are grasping at things or looking into an imagined future. Nature is in the moment. Being awake and aware of each moment, letting go of desires and wants, lets you enjoy and accept everything just as it is.

Plan to rise one hour earlier for a week. Consider your extra hour a personal bonus, and use it for the things you usually don't have time for: meditation, yoga, or taking a walk and noticing how different everything appears before the day's routines have taken hold.

Full of vitamins B6 and C and potassium, bananas are health-giving as well as wonderfully portable and in other ways convenient. (They could almost have been designed for picnics.) Cultivated bananas turn from green to yellow to indicate when they are ripe for eating. Some have cited the banana as a convincing argument for a divinely-made universe—the epitome of intelligent design. Whatever your beliefs, rejoice in this mini-miracle of natural packaging.

Cherish others, and the sun of real happiness will shine in your life.

Try this experiment: Stand before a mirror in your bathroom, first looking into the reflection. You are looking and the reflection is the object. Then change the whole situation, reversing the process. Start feeling that you are the reflection and the reflection is looking at you. Immediately you will see a change happening, a great energy moving toward you. If you do this for a few days, you will be surprised by how much more alive you feel the whole day. There is an energy circle taking place, and whenever the circle is complete, there is a great silence. This silence makes you centered, and to be centered is to be powerful. You can also do this with a flower, tree, or star instead of a mirror.

Pick a handful of different leaves. Sit and really study them, the shapes, colors, and textures. Feel their temperature. Trace the veins with your fingers. Meditate on the patterns you see. Close your eyes and smell the leaves. Become completely absorbed in the leaves.

Leave behind destructive reactions and become as patient as the earth.

Ancient sites of ritual, from the stone circles of northern Europe to the medicine wheels of Native North America, emit powerful but subtle energies. What better places to perform your own personal rituals, perhaps a rain dance, a prayer for peace, or a thanks-giving for the unfolding of history which makes the present moment flower. At the very least, be alert to the ancient energies of the stones and imbibe the peace in which they have rested for so many centuries.

At bedtime, imagine that you are lost in a mountainous region. It is a very dark night and there is no moon in the sky and it is cloudy, so you cannot see a single star. You are lost and it is dark. There are many dangers. You are fully alert because the danger is tremendous. Even if a pin drops, you will be able to hear it. Suddenly you come near a precipice. There is no way to go ahead. You do not know how deep the abyss is so you throw a rock into it to see how deep it is. You wait and listen for the rock to hit below. You continue listening, but the rock never hits the bottom. It is utterly silent. In that silence, fall asleep.

The wind cannot overturn a mountain, but it can overturn a frail tree.

Imagine a safe, protected, peaceful place, maybe somewhere in a forest or on a beach. Experience this place fully and with all of your senses. Note how calm and relaxed you feel throughout your body. Carry this feeling with you when you end the visualization exercise.

To instill awareness of the impermanence of existence, Tibetan Buddhists create intricate sand mandalas, which are then ritually destroyed. The sand is collected in a glass vessel and released back into nature by being poured into a lake or stream. Inscribe an intricate sand mandala next time you're on the beach as the tide is coming in. Meditate on time as the tide washes over your design: vow to accept the passing moments as they occur.

Do a sea-tumbling relaxation exercise. Lie down in a comfortable place with your arms and legs flopped out naturally. Imagine lying at the sea's edge on an empty beach. The tide is coming in. Gentle waves lap your feet and ankles and very slowly move up your body until you are bathed in shallow water. As the water rises, sense yourself starting to float and being drawn by the rhythmic currents out to sea. Feel the waves beneath you as you glide over their peaks and troughs. Physically, turn over onto your front. Now imagine riding the crest of a wave and arriving back on the shore on smooth, warm sand. Stay here and experience the profound calm induced by the meditation.

Friendly support acts like the soil so the seed in the person can grow.

Take a walk at night, carefully and stealthily, pretending you are an animal. Be in a super-alert state and seek out the darkest areas. Relish the darkness and your life as an animal. You can even try closing your eyes and walking in the dark with the aid of a friend.

The companionship we humans can share with pets is a testament to our ability to love and communicate beyond intellect, beyond shared interests, and beyond the ties of family. Take time to get to know one or two animals, building a bond of mutual trust. Spiritual kinship outside our peer group brings profound rewards. Animals can be refreshing company, not least in their lack of pretension and their unembarrassed playfulness and affection.

Spring-clean your brain any time of year and learn how to pay attention.

When you eat a tangerine, eat it with awareness. When you peel it, know you are peeling it. When you remove a slice, and put it in your mouth, know that you are removing a slice and putting it in your mouth. When you experience its fragrance and sweet taste, be aware that you are experiencing its fragrance and sweet taste. Eat each morsel with awareness. You see the tangerine tree, the tangerine blossom, and the sunlight and rain which nurtured the tree. You see tons of things which have made the tangerine possible. Looking at a tangerine with awareness you can see all the wonders of the universe and how all things interact with each other.

Celebrate the summer by organizing an outdoor party for everyone who lives on your street, on your block, or in your apartment building. There may well be a wide variety of races, ages, and backgrounds present. Marvel at the diversity within a relatively small area.

Waking up to a beautiful day naturally lifts our spirits, but scientists at the University of Michigan have found that in order to fully benefit from the mood-enhancing properties of good weather, we each need to spend at least thirty minutes outside, a tall order if you've a busy day ahead. Next time the sun is shining, plan a half-hour of appreciation: take your lunch to the park, or include walking time in your journey to work.

Sometimes you are stuck inside. Here is a meditation to connect you with nature even when you do not have access to nature because of the weather, being at work, or for some other reason. Start by looking out a window that has the widest possible view. Notice the seasonal features. If you can open the window, you can sniff and see what natural scents you pick up. Listen for sounds of nature, even if you are in an urban landscape. Make this a regular practice in situations where you must be inside. Try to stop and look outside or take advantage of websites or device apps that show nature scenes coupled with nature sounds.

Flowers grow on their own. Doing nothing is very often more than enough.

If you watch how a baby breathes, you will see the whole musculature of the abdomen completely open and participate in the breathing process. You want to practice this, breathing just like a baby, deeply into the belly and chest, naturally—as you were born to do.

The development from chrysalis to butterfly is a potent and universal symbol of personal change, reminding us that our power to transform ourselves lies within. Butterflies also suggest the fragile intensity of life's beauty. When you see a butterfly landing on a flower, know that your work toward positive personal change can bring fulfillment.

See yourself lying on a patch of thick, fragrant, green grass on a hillside mildly sloping under an old elm tree. The sky is spotted with full, bulging, white clouds that float slowly across the blue. The air's temperature is the same as your skin's temperature. You take many deep breaths, concentrating on how relaxing they are. See and feel yourself float into your surroundings, looking all around. Travel to different places such as a forest or beach. Float there. Look. Smell. Experience. When you are ready to end the journey, imagine yourself back on the hillside under the elm tree. It is now sunset. Take another deep breath and remember what you felt.

Do something peaceful, magical, and serene in the evening. Go for a walk before dinner, light candles or incense, take a long bath, prepare dinner in a ritualized manner, or just sit and meditate. Take the time to release the day's cares, tensions, and stresses.

Feed your body and mind with good food. Try natural, organic foods.

Forgetfulness is the opposite of mindfulness. You drink a cup of tea, but you are not in the moment drinking a cup of tea. You sit with the person you love, but you do not know they are there. You walk in nature, but you are not really paying attention. You are someplace else, thinking about the past or the future. The horse of your habit energy carries you along like a captive. You need to stop the horse and reclaim your freedom.

Japanese rock gardens classically contain just stones and fine gravel. Careful attention is paid to the specific placement of the rocks, and the gravel is raked to suggest rippling water. Such gardens are designed to act as a meditation aid when viewed from a seat nearby. Construct your own mini rock garden next time you have the opportunity, perhaps in your own backyard, at the beach, or even inside the house. Once you've chosen a formation for your rocks and sand, rake a pattern and sit quietly in meditation, focusing on the design as if it were a three-dimensional mandala. Afterward, relax and meditate. Read a haiku or two.

Smile at both the flower and the garbage and you will embrace both.

In a dish of pet food, see the presence of the entire universe supporting the existence of your animal. Be grateful to have food to serve your animal. This feeding is a show of love and respect. Animals teach you all about unconditional love and gratitude.

The garden is an image of Paradise, an open-air setting in which nature and art are in balance. Any spiritual discipline performed in a garden—yoga, tai chi, meditation, or even prayer, gains from the open air and harmonious environment. Or you can simply relax there, with eyes closed, treating your senses to lovely sounds and smells. Wind chimes in a garden add the music of the breeze—gentle, random, and deeply soothing.

We are all inescapably confined to the body and mind we inhabit, and it's pointless to wish it were otherwise. However, imagining how things would appear from another perspective gives us fresh insights that can help to break down the walls of habitual thinking. Spend five minutes imagining that you're a cat. Curl up in a ball among a pile of cushions on the floor. With eyes closed, breathe deeply. Listen attentively to every sound. What would you be thinking if this transformation were for real? What would you be anticipating? What would you be afraid of? Try this exercise with other creatures, too. For example, a spider, a goldfish, or a sparrow.

The flower that blooms for only a single night is indeed a sight to behold.

Meditate on the sky, especially a sky with no clouds, endlessly empty and clear, nothing moving in it. Contemplate it, meditate on it, and enter this clarity. Become this clarity. Do this lying down so you can forget the earth. Don't think about the sky; observe.

The aurora borealis, or northern lights, is a spectacular, sublime phenomenon of the polar night skies, a wide curtain of green, blue, or red light shimmering like a ghostly theatrical effect. The cause is complex; it results from the reaction of the solar winds with earth's magnetic field in certain conditions. If you can, go on a northern lights safari within the Arctic circle and enjoy the light show of a lifetime.

Caring for a living creature teaches you responsibility and loving-kindness.

Chakra meditation: Sit cross-legged, take three deep breaths, then breathe naturally. Using your mind, try to sense the chakra at the base of your spine. You can imagine it as a lotus flower or as a spinning wheel or storehouse of energy. Sense the energy. Move up to the next chakra in the lower abdomen, just above your genital area. Feel its energy. You can breathe energy into the chakra, revitalizing it. Move up to the chakra in the solar plexus/navel, then the heart, then the throat, then the forehead between the eyes, and finally to the top of your head. Think about what each chakra feels like, the energy of each. Relax and take deep breaths to finish.

For walking meditation: Recognize that your mind can and does go in a thousand directions. Right now, walk in one direction and keep your mind with your steps or breath also in one direction. Each step creates peace. With each step, imagine that a lotus blooms.

"One of the reasons we love the seaside is that so many things invite us into the present moment: the sound of waves crashing on the shore, the flight of seagulls, the moist, salty air, and the feel of sand between our toes. By bringing attention to our moment-to-moment experience, the beach can be a wonderful place to practice mindfulness, and by doing so, enhance our joy and appreciation of the present." —Mark Coleman, mindfulness teacher and author of *Make Peace with Your Mind*

In nature there are neither rewards nor punishments; there are only consequences.

Imagine a bubble of bright yellow sunlight all around you. You are safe inside. The bubble of sun is charged with sparkling, protective energy. It moves with you and though it is soft on the inside, on the outside it is strong and shielding you from whatever makes you anxious. It is keeping whatever worries you at a distance. While you are inside the sunlight bubble, focus on your breathing. Visualize the sun's light flowing in and out of your pores as you inhale and exhale. The sparkling light is filling you with strength and energy. Keep the bubble around you until the pressure has subsided and you feel comfortable enough to let it go.

Consider a problem within a larger context. Imagine you are in the sky, a bird soaring, looking down at the problem far below. It will likely seem insignificant on this scale, and your anxiety about it should diminish. Return to earth ready to face the problem.

In solitude you gain peace and balance, like the wind not caught by any net.

In beauty, scent, and form the rose is the queen of flowers. It also has a many-layered symbolism with connotations of love and sacrifice. Italian poet Dante compared heavenly love with the heart of a rose, while the Austrian poet Rilke wrote of the petals as the eyelids of a sleepless eternal being. Wear a rose sprig in your lapel or in your hat, and pull it out from time to time to relish its beauty and ponder its symbolism.

Try a practice when you are outside to gauge how many pleasant things you notice as well as how many unpleasant things you sense in your environment. Are you in the moment or thinking about what might go wrong while you are outside, or thinking about something you should be doing inside? This practice is intended to help you see where your mind naturally dwells. Are you seeking the positive or dwelling on the negative? Are you in the moment or fretting about the future or rehashing the past? Being mindful of the focus of your attention can be a great way to adopt a more positive, present way of behaving in other situations.

Feel an intimate connection with earth and a reverential concern for nature.

As the sun goes down and the sky changes color, walk toward the sun and follow it on the horizon. Notice the sky and light's changes. Say goodbye or good night to the sun. Acknowledge that the day and yourself have changed. Look forward to the sunrise tomorrow.

The cow is a fascinating creature, rich in associations. Traditionally, crescent horns represent the moon, while the udder suggests the Milky Way, so the cow combines lunar and stellar symbolism. To drink cow's milk is an affirmation of a wonderful symbiotic or mutually beneficial relationship. Think of the cow when the world seems all too familiar, its quintessential strangeness is a tonic for jaded perceptions.

Visualize your whole body and mind as being filled with total darkness. Feel the sadness without being overwhelmed by it. Prepare to invoke healing light. Imagine the light coming from your source of power within you, in front of you, or from above. See the beams of light, bright, warm, and joyful. The light fills your entire body, penetrating each and every cell. Imagine the light shining beyond your body, lighting the whole world and universe. Feel the nature of the healing light. It is not solid and cannot be held. It is just light. You and the universe are sharing this light. It is ethereal and can disappear and reappear at any time.

Shovel snow and jump in the pile. Combine work with fun, just like nature does. On a shoreline, collect some rocks, pebbles, or shells. Think of habits, fears, resentments, and beliefs you are ready to let go of. When you are ready, toss a rock, pebble, or shell into the water and let it carry with it the negative feeling you are ready to let go of.

Water is vital for life, and the only substance that is commonly found in three different states: ice, water, and vapor. At the symbolic level, water stands for unconscious energy, the formless powers of spirit, and pure nature following its own way without interference. Pile ice cubes into a glass and meditate on them till they melt to a pool. This state of pure being is all the soul is and all the soul needs.

Understand that you are a continuum. A simple piece of fruit is a continuum. It is a fusion of many things and many moments. Allow your continuum to unfold in balance, joy, and peace.

Power breath: Begin by going for a walk, preferably alone and outside. Inhale, silently saying *Om* to the count of two. Mentally see that the oxygen coming into your body is filled with life-force energy and hold the breath in your mouth. As you force the air against your cheeks, let them fill to capacity and bulge out. Keep pressing the air into your cheeks as long as you can, without creating discomfort. Then exhale to the count of seven. Repeat this twelve times. Try doing this twice a day, gradually increasing to hold your breath for five counts and exhale for ten counts, then hold your breath outside for five counts.

In walking meditation, keep your mind totally focused on your environment, not on the thoughts that try to distract you. Notice a thought, return to the walking, notice a thought, return to the walking. Let go of all thoughts and allow whatever emerges to be.

Like a monkey in the forest you jump from tree to tree, never finding the fruit.

A major challenge might seem like a river in flood that blocks your path. You can't judge the depth of the water, so you stand there, panicked, wondering what to do. Don't just charge in. Instead, spend a few minutes looking carefully to see whether stepping stones are visible just below the water's surface. Often, they are. Pick your way across the stones calmly and carefully. The obstacle may be less formidable than you feared.

Since we are all connected in this ocean of life, everything we do comes back to us.

Begin your walk with your whole body attentive to experience. Feel the temperature of the air on your skin. If there is a breeze, feel it press against you. Smell the air. Listen to the sounds around you. Imagine that your eyes are a wide-angle camera lens and let them receive a panoramic view. Feel your whole body moving through space. Notice how all parts of the body are naturally, unselfconsciously involved. No planning is needed for walking. Walking happens. Feel the walk with your whole body. Attend to the bodily sensations and move your focus to different parts to help you maintain composure. Stay alert.

Notice the ocean and its waves. Think about the waves of your life in that context.

When you are walking in nature, you can smile and say hello to what you see, hear, and come into contact with. Smile at a pebble you happen to step on. Smile at the sky, the trees, the wind. With a smile, you can feel your breath and your steps more clearly.

The long, straight horizon of the ocean is wonderfully calming, especially in a tropical paradise. It's a good subject for a relaxing visualization. But it's also a reminder of the miracle of the elements: the earth beneath your feet, the sky and water dominating your view, and the sun—if you're lucky—shining on everything. Relish this elemental experience whenever you get the chance to walk on the shore.

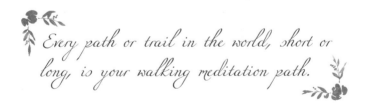

Every path or trail in the world, short or long, is your walking meditation path.

Kinhin (walking meditation) is performed by placing the right fist, with thumb inside, on the chest and covering it with the left palm while holding both palms at right angles. Keep the arms in a straight line and the body erect, eyes resting on a point about six feet in front of the feet. At the same time, continue to count inhalations and exhalations as you walk slowly around a room. Begin walking with the left foot and walk in such a way that the foot sinks into the floor, first the heel and then the toes. Walk calmly and steadily, with poise and dignity. Think of this walking as zazen or sitting meditation in motion.

Take a stone or pebble and drop it in a still lake or pond. Notice how it affects the place where it entered as well as how it created ripples spreading from that spot. Just as the water is fluid and connected, so is life. Each action affects the whole.

With your understanding of the interconnectedness of nature with human beings, ask yourself what it is you can do to help preserve, protect, and support the natural world. Are there ways that your choices or lifestyle or even your work causes harm to nature? Devise a change you can make or a project you can start or become involved with to bring your life into more harmony with nature.

Pearl diving in the south seas used to be a hazardous operation, which helped to give the pearl its mystique. Not every oyster has its pearl; this gem is formed only when a microscopic stowaway infiltrates the mollusk's shell, causing the creature to secrete layers of pearly armor around the irritant. Unsurprisingly, the pearl became a metaphor for something rare and precious. Meditate on a pearl earring or necklace and reflect on how beauty is often the accidental result of function, like the spirit, when focused on love and compassion, flowers into pearl-like majesty.

Curling up with a cat or walking the dog can create a naturally meditative state.

Stand by a body of still or calm water, like a lake or pond, or even a puddle. Note that underneath and above there is undetectable movement. Internalize this feeling of stillness and let it calm you. Feel your heart slowing and your mind growing still.

The stained-glass window is a beautiful invention of the Gothic style of architecture. On a sunny day, the play of tinted light in a shadowy interior is heartwarming, the visual equivalent of heavenly music, while the panes themselves glow with saturated hues. Surrender to such visual harmony whenever you have the opportunity. Light transforming glass is an image of the miraculous spirit transforming a human life.

Try a sanctuary meditation. See yourself in a natural setting with all of the details of sight, sound, and smell. Feel comfortable and relaxed in the setting. Ahead, you will see a clearing. When you get to the clearing, lie down and relax in the sun. You are safe and you can stay as long as you like. You may now meet your meditative guide and enter a glade of trees. You may converse with your guide about everyday or spiritual matters. When you have finished, thank your guide and make your way out of the clearing and back to the natural setting. Finish by opening your eyes.

On a warm day, take the opportunity to sit outside in the sun, on a chair, or on the ground with your eyes closed. Feel the warmth bathing you. Connect the sun's energy to your core. Visualize a warm yellow glow spreading to fill the rest of your body.

The journey of the Atlantic salmon from the far wilderness of the ocean back to the river of its own birth and upstream to spawn is one of the wonders of nature, and a fitting emblem of persistence and sacrifice (the trek is exhausting and few survive). Ask yourself what sacrifices will be required of you on your journey through life. Perhaps any suffering you have experienced is part of your destiny.

Take a one-minute vacation just before you get in the car or onto the train, walk the dog, start your shower, or begin work. Pause for a minute and stand still. Look around and just notice the nature, taking a photo with your eyes. Breathe deeply, then close your eyes and listen. Note the feel of the air, sun, or wind. Connect with nature in this way for a few one-minute sessions each day. Think of all the places and times you can take this pause. Note how you feel about this practice once you start doing it. Do you look forward to it and find excuses to do it?

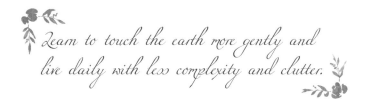

Learn to touch the earth more gently and live daily with less complexity and clutter.

Contemplate the ways humankind exploits animals. Contemplate the many species lost. Embrace all animals with your compassion. Wish for your compassion to ease their suffering. Protect life, practice generosity, behave responsibly, and consume mindfully.

A walk outside will help you reconnect with the natural world. A Zen-like concept is to walk a mile in another person's shoes. Whenever you catch yourself making "us" and "them" distinctions or criticisms, spend a moment being the other person. Put yourself in his or her shoes. It may change your perspective and help you find tolerance, even compassion, toward someone you didn't understand.

Live in accord with nature and follow a proper life and you will want for nothing.

Mandala meditation: With open eyes, jog in place, faster and faster, raising your knees up. Breathe deeply and evenly. Forget everything else and keep going for ten to fifteen minutes. Then sit with your eyes closed and mouth loose and open. Gently rotate your body from the waist like a reed blowing in the wind. Feel the wind blowing you side to side, back and forth, around and around. Do this for ten to fifteen minutes. Then lie on your back, eyes open, and with the head still, rotate your eyes clockwise for a few minutes. Finally, close your eyes and be still for a time.

When you are in nature, feel the power of the sun, wind, trees, plants, and animals around you. Bring awareness to your body. When you sit, know you are sitting. When you eat, know you are eating. When you walk, feel the sensations of the body walking.

The unenlightened soul looks at existence through a keyhole. A form might pass by—a person, an animal, a rain cloud—and we merely glimpse it as it passes. Enlightenment, achievable through profound meditation, admits us through the keyhole into the true nature of the cosmos. Your view will be partial until you broaden your vision by accessing the spirit and the One.

Align with nature and accept today's weather, whatever it is. This acceptance is needed for life.

Imagine that your mind is the trunk of a tree and all your thoughts are branches. The strong branches with green leaves represent healthy mind states, while withered, dying branches are distracting emotions, feelings, and thoughts. Visualize yourself reaching up to the branches of distraction and cutting them off the tree. Then let go of each distraction. You may gently note and label each distraction as you cut it down and let it go. Promise yourself that from now on, whenever a distraction enters your mind, you will see it, acknowledge it, then let it go.

Go out while it is raining and imagine that you are a tree. Receive the rain as the tree would. Feel the rain nourish you. Then dance or move in any way you feel natural to allow yourself to rejoice in the nourishment and the beauty of the water cycle.

The rainforest is a byword for biodiversity, and many of its species of plant, insect, and animal are still unrecorded. The rainforest is the planet's natural pharmacy, as well as its lungs and its bestiary. Add your voice to the chorus of protest as the rainforest is cleared by loggers and developers. The health of the planet is measured as much by the fate of the rainforest as of the icecaps.

Nature is simply being. Emulate this as often as you can. Be satisfied in the being.

Visualize a butterfly inside your heart. Gently, it opens its wings. Breathe deeply and slowly, imagining the breath flowing into the butterfly. Sense the compassion and love growing. Let the butterfly fly out into the world with compassion and love.

The planet Venus is sometimes the morning star, and sometimes the evening star. There are also times when Venus disappears completely, hidden behind the sun. Locate Venus in the sky around sunset; not far from the sun itself, she will usually be unmissable, the brightest heavenly body in the sky. Meditate quietly, allowing the planet's purity, clarity, and tranquility to enter your soul.

Seat yourself outside or by an open window facing the sun. This is a natural light energy meditation. The sun is an inexhaustible fountain of energy. Breathe in its energy through all the pores of your body. Even if a cloud obscures it, know that the sun's rays are reaching you and nourishing you. Natural light is so much more important than artificial light, yet we often spend more time in the latter. Use this meditation to cultivate appreciation of natural light.

When you walk outdoors, notice all the life surrounding you. Feel the magic of life, including your own self, with all of your senses. Note that you are not alone. Everything is connected in the web of life. You can never feel lonesome knowing this.

In Aztec mythology, god Huitzilopochtli uses the weapon of sunlight to drive away the creatures of darkness, the stars and the moon, from the sky every day. Learn from this warrior of illumination: Any time dark or negative thoughts enter your mind, recognize them as your enemy and visualize a sword of bright light chasing them away. Make your mind a sanctuary for sunny, positive thoughts.

Be aware of the fragile and impermanent nature of all life, including your own.

In the Eastern religion of Jainism, every living being has a soul; Jain monks and nuns walk barefoot, sweeping the ground ahead to avoid injuring even the tiniest creatures. When insects invade your home, exercise compassion in gently removing them. They too have their role in the wider cosmos.

When you get angry, don't react or speak. Remain mum and unmoved, like a tree.

To do pure love meditation, focus on some person or animal you feel great love and affection for. You must have a strong heart connection with this being. Picture the person or animal clearly in your mind and imagine him or her giving you a look that melts your heart. Think about the things you most love and appreciate about this being. You can even imagine giving a warm, heartfelt hug to them. With each breath, let your heart be filled with the love and affection you feel. Imagine your two souls connected by the caring you have for each other.

When outside, look for the first animal to cross your path. Watch how it takes in its environment. Tell it that you want to understand it better and maybe be its friend. Watch and learn. Say goodbye when it leaves. Later, reflect on the encounter.

Hard-edged shadows remind us of the wonder of sunlight, which travels more than 90 million miles in perfect straight lines. The sun's yellow color is caused by the scattering of shorter wavelengths of violet and blue light. When the sun is low in the sky, more light is scattered, causing the color to deepen to orange or red. Next time you see a glowing sunset, relish this knowledge.

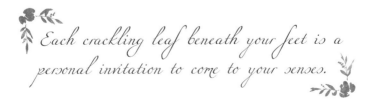

Each crackling leaf beneath your feet is a personal invitation to come to your senses.

Do a beach chair meditation: Lean back in a comfy beach chair or chaise lounge with legs outstretched, and totally relax. Let go of body and mind; let go, and let goodness in. At the poolside, on your patio or porch, in a garden, or on the beach, raise your gaze and open your eyes and heart and mind. Elevate the scope of global, 365-degree panoramic awareness. Simply relax and watch the rolling waves of sea or river or the clouds pass by while the mind unfurls, as the soul unfolds, as the infinite sky opens up, revealing the joy of meditation.

On a rainy day, find a sheltered place outside or sit inside by an open window. Close your eyes and breathe deeply three times. Become present with the natural sounds of the water on objects like leaves, roads, and structures. Focus on the sounds.

Whenever you build a fire, use wood that has fallen rather than cutting live branches.

Remember your objectives in meditation: you want to achieve a state of complete physical stillness, yet you do not want to fall asleep. You want to promote a totally settled state of the body which will engender a corresponding mental settling. There must also be a state of physical alertness which can induce the kind of mental clarity you seek.

Select an object of nature to involve in this practice. You can choose a stone, tree, body of water, or clouds. Water and leaves are constantly moving and changing, so they are ideal partners for meditation practices. With water, let your mind stay present with the water, moment to moment. If your mind wanders off into thoughts, bring the mind gently back to what the water is doing. With a plant, flower, leaves, or tree, let your eyes rest on the object as it is, moment to moment. Stay present with the light, patterns, shapes, and movement.

Think only and entirely of what you are doing in the moment and you are free as a bird.

Standing meditation is learned best from trees. When you are standing alone, open your palms to the sky and hold your arms out like branches, open and patient. Stand still like the trees; they are not lost.

The impermanence of all things is a key concept in Buddhist teachings. Life embodies this in our aging, in the cycle of life, death, and rebirth, and in our experience of loss. Much of our suffering stems from denying impermanence or clinging to the impermanent as if it's going to last forever. Don't view age like this; let the years pass away, like rain into the earth.

Say nothing and saw wood. Do not react or speak—be like a tree—rest like a great tree.

Affirmation exercise: bring your attention to your breathing, which should be natural. When you feel ready, repeat the word *relax* to yourself, either silently or out loud. Say the first syllable *re* as you breathe in and second syllable *lax* as you breathe out. Do not try to force your breathing into a rhythm or pattern, just keep breathing normally and match the speed of the affirmation to the breathing. When your mind wanders, bring it back gently and continue to repeat the word *relax*. Repeat this exercise for as long as it feels comfortable.

Bring awareness to walking wherever you are. Slow down a bit, centering yourself in the present moment in your body. Appreciate the fact that you are able to walk. This is not something to take for granted. Walk with dignity and confidence.

The best rewards are not easily won. If a project seems to be taking forever to come to fruition, imagine yourself as a farmer: preparing the ground, sowing the seeds, caring for them as they grow, and finally harvesting the fruit of your hard labor. Work intensively, involving yourself fully in every stage of your project, and you'll appreciate the results all the more.

Eating an orange: Place an orange on a plate and close your eyes. Let go of all thoughts and preconceptions. Open your eyes and see the fruit as if for the first time. Begin to peel the orange and see how it feels: the texture, the weight. Slowly raise a piece of the orange to your lips. Be sure to smell it. Pause for a moment before eating. Open your mouth, bite down, and feel the texture and juice in your mouth. Continue to bite and chew the orange piece thoroughly before picking up another piece.

The power of patience is seen in the effect of many drops of water onto a rock over time.

Find a beach where you can sit peacefully. On each inhale, feel the warmth of the sun and sand and the touch of the breeze. Let your breathing coincide with the rhythm of the waves. Feel tension releasing from your body during each exhale.

Benevolence is silent good will streaming out indiscriminately into the world and into your life. Think of the sun shining in winter, softening the earth, melting the ice; it gives without design or intention to heal. The ground feels no debt to the sun; neither does the sun expect gratitude. Follow the way of benevolence, which is always well lit, even on the darkest night.

Take a few moments to experience the sensation of simply standing still outside on grass, sand, a patio, or porch. Stand barefoot with your feet shoulder-width apart, stomach muscles engaged, and the rest of your body relaxed. Spread your toes widely to feel a sense of connection with the earth. Visualize roots growing downward from your feet. At the same time, imagine there's a fine thread pulling you upward from the crown of your head. Enjoy these opposing but complementary feelings of deep stability and graceful lightness.

Meditate and visualize yourself on a tropical beach. On each inhale, feel the warmth of the sun and the touch of the breeze. Let your breathing coincide with the rhythm of the waves. Feel tension release from your body during each exhale.

Try to be mindful and let things take their natural course. Then your mind will become still in any surroundings, like a still forest pool. All kinds of wonderful animals will come to drink at the pool and you will clearly see the nature of all things. You will see many strange and wonderful things come and go, but you will be still. This is the happiness of the Buddha.

Meditate when you are on an airplane. There is not really a better situation than to meditate at a high altitude. When gravitation is less and the earth's pull is less, when you are surrounded by clouds and space, this is a natural thing to meditate. For a few minutes, sit with your eyes closed and feel that you are becoming bigger and filling the plane. Then feel that you grow bigger than the plane until you have expanded to the whole sky. The clouds and moon and stars are moving within you.

Meditate on a recent weather event you experienced. Perhaps it was a still, cloudy morning that gave way to a sunny, windy afternoon. Perhaps it was a thunderstorm washing away all the dirt and humid air, leaving the air clean and crisp.

Your spiritual side may suffer from neglect if you're busy with childcare, or a profession, or simply trying to make ends meet. To give yourself a quick reminder of the deeper things of life, visualize a lotus blossom floating on a pond. Imagine light streaming out from the flower's petals. Let the light fill you with calm radiance and bring harmony back to your life.

Try to find time during the middle of the day for walking meditation, preferably outdoors.

At the end of every exhalation and inhalation, your body experiences a natural pause called an apnea, from the Greek meaning "without breathing." This is a state of bodily equilibrium, when all your breathing structures relax. Bring your attention to your breathing, and detect these natural pauses. Can you elongate them, without straining your breath? There's a distinct quality of peaceful awareness to these pauses. See if you can find this natural stillness, and leave your mind there as you continue breathing normally.

Look carefully at an object such as a leaf or the bark on a tree. Allow your gaze to soften as you explore the object. Observe the colors, shape, and texture. Look for details you might have missed at first glance. Become truly curious.

While on hold on the telephone, think about this: does a dog or cat have a spiritual nature?

Happiness cannot be found through great effort and willpower. It is already present, in open relaxation and letting go. Cultivating mindfulness teaches us to calm down enough to enter and dwell in states of deep relaxation. Watching television, for example, hardly ever promotes physiological or psychological relaxation, but taking a walk through a natural area does.

Sit beneath a tree with your back resting against it for support. Perhaps you'll want a blanket or item of clothing to sit on. Try to face east or north. East is the direction in which the sun rises. It is the source of light and the source of life itself. The north is determined by the polar star, the symbol of stability; it is the fixed goal that never wavers. Facing north helps you find and follow your right direction. Sit comfortably in a meditation position with your eyes closed or open for at least twenty minutes.

Consider the changing seasons and how there could never be new growth without decay and death.

Silence is a natural mindfulness practice. It is a refuge and a teacher. Silence is the nurturing ground of the soul. If you can achieve a quality of true silence in your life, awareness will bubble up like spring water from the earth.

In some Far Eastern cultures, a lunar eclipse is believed to be caused by a dragon swallowing the moon. Our understanding is always colored by the culture we inhabit. Even today's Western science is an approximation; on its own terms, it leaves much unexplained. True reality lies beyond understanding. True awareness knows reality directly, as a mystic knows God.

There is a great ancient tradition of meditating with trees. Find a tree you would like to commune with. Ask the tree if you can enter into a friendship. Stand like the tree and embrace it. Feel the tree embracing you in return. Relax and let go of tensions you may have been feeling. The tree is centered, grounded, rooted. It is one with the sky above and the earth below. Close your eyes and let your spirit feel the healing energy of the tree. Trust what is happening and surrender to what the tree can teach you.

With each weed you pull up, you make room for fresh green grass. Prune the garden of your mind.

When practicing meditation outside in a public place, keep your eyes open to take in the environment. Just look anywhere and rest your eyes on something beautiful that soothes you. Look. Really look. Breathe in the abundance.

Changing our eating habits is challenging but not impossible. See the beauty of nature and how food is grown. Get involved in the growing, picking, and preparation of wholesome foods. See the interconnectedness between yourself and food. When you eat something delicious and healthy that you had a part in creating, you develop a more positive relationship with food.

Kind hearts are gardens, kind thoughts are roots, kind words are flowers, kind deeds are fruits.

Find a quiet place outside where you can comfortably touch the earth with your feet. Feel the weight of your body through your feet and toes and the pressure points. Note the temperature, density, and resistance of the ground. Sink into the ground and begin walking slowly. Note the changes in what you feel. Then, after a few minutes, stop and touch the ground with your hands. Play with it. Then continue your walk. At the end of your walk, take some time to sit and breathe in the sunlight or under a tree.

Make every attempt to leave your mind in its present, natural state, without thinking about what happened in the past or what could happen in the future. Let thoughts flow through, until your mind becomes like clear, still water.

Think that your life is as interesting and miraculous as the stars and the moon and the universe.

A globe of the world is a representation of the miracle you were born into; a planet which, when seen from space by astronauts, unfailingly inspires love. Spin a globe slowly, as if you yourself were in orbit. Imagine seven billion souls, showing courage, compassion, or forgiveness in countless ways, or suffering in war or poverty. Resolve to help where you can.

We speak of losing ourselves in profound and absorbing experiences. Take this idea literally and visit somewhere completely new to you like a stretch of countryside or a state park with a lookout to climb to. Use a map to plan a walk, and set off with refreshments. At a certain point, tuck the map away and walk from memory. When you become disoriented, relish this liberating sensation. Appreciate what you discover. In unfamiliar territory, we can learn how to see again.

Early in the morning before anyone else is up, go outside and look—really, mindfully, look—at the stars, moon, light coming up. Feel the air, the temperature, the moisture in the air; mindfully feeling. Then sit and meditate.

Think of the generative power of nature, the way new life is conjured from seeds and other small beginnings. Then turn your mind to the power of your own thoughts, which is no less astonishing. You have the infinite capacity to spin one idea out of another. You are the emperor of the realm of thought—as potentially powerful as anyone who ever lived.

In falling asleep, focus on your breath. Then transfer your awareness to your heart. You may be aware of it beating or you may just focus on the space of the heart. Visualize and try to sense the presence of a disk of still white light with its center at the heart and its circumference extending a little beyond the heart. Set the disk spinning, slowly and then faster. As it spins, visualize a rainbow of colors and their merging to form the white light. Fall asleep with the disk still spinning.

Feelings are as ephemeral as the weather. Meditation allows you to ride out the storms gracefully.

The next time you find yourself at a lake, pond, river, or ocean, listen to the white sound of the water. Enter into the flow of the water and let it wash everything away. Let all your thoughts fall into the water and dissolve.

Witnessing an eclipse can be an astonishing experience. As the shadow of earth starts to edge across the sun or the moon, the sheer scale of the phenomenon can be unsettling, as can the realization that our lives depend on a fine cosmic balance. What better time to give thanks for the grand universal system in which we're privileged to have a place.

The real storm is inside you, as is the calm that follows when you realize that everything is fine.

Sit in a chair outside and take a few moments to become aware of how gravity acts on your body. Notice the weight of your legs and hips against the chair. Stand up and notice how gravity pulls you toward the earth. Begin walking and pay attention to the tug of gravity in each footstep. Notice how everything around you is held in place by gravity. You move through a field of gravity like a fish swimming through water. Try to be aware of this invisible field as you go through your day.

As you meditate, imagine yourself opening a door to a field of wildflowers that leads to a higher level of awareness. As you open the door, sunlight floods in to feed the wildflowers. Visualize walking into this brighter place.

As you dig through your emotions and beliefs, examine each find carefully, brushing the dirt away and taking care to uncover all its features before making a decision about its worth. Don't cling to valueless, outdated junk because you're attached to it; you risk inhibiting personal growth. But be careful to keep intact your most treasured thoughts.

A meditation for releasing fear: Close your eyes and bring to mind one of your deepest fears. Acknowledge the presence of your fear. Be aware of its existence and observe how it feels without getting caught up in it or judging yourself for having this fear. Now imagine the fear as a caged bird and give it an appearance. Then imagine opening the cage and setting the bird free. As you watch the bird fly away, you are releasing the fear from your consciousness. Accept this feeling.

Create an island of "being" in the sea of constant "doing," in which your life is usually immersed.

Make your own miniature Zen garden. It can be the focus of meditation. Choose the garden's objects with care, using items from nature and placing them in sand in a shallow dish. Create wavelike patterns in the sand around the objects.

Chinese landscape paintings often include tiny figures, as if to emphasize the grandeur of nature, of which humankind is one small part. Think of the world in these terms, as larger in scale than the human. This is a healthy corrective to the commonplace view that people own the land, which exists to serve their purposes. Think big and live small.

For a week, take some time each day to do something outdoors that is fun, joyful, or pleasurable for you. Maybe it is just sitting outside with your cat on your lap, riding your bike to the beach, or sitting on your stoop to view the night sky. Be sure to notice the joy, whatever makes you happy and lifts your spirits when you are outdoors. When these feelings come, savor them, and you'll see how these positive feelings will carry over to your day when you step back inside.

Earth yoga poses offer grounding energy. Examples of earth poses are lotus, half lotus, tree, and mountain.

Go to a garden and just stand in it. Breathe in the air, the fragrances, the light, the temperature, and the music of the plant and animal life. Inhale the energy of these growing things. Recharge your spirit and inner batteries.

A pebble in your pocket or another item from nature can serve as a teacher, a reminder for when you slip into autopilot and lose awareness. A reminder like this can teach you to pause and return to your breathing. Beginning again is an important part of practice and is one of the great builders of mindfulness. It is always okay to begin again.

Take a long walk in nature without a set plan or path. That way, you will have to be more open to whatever happens, not knowing what to expect. As you walk, pay attention to the surprises along the way. When you reach a place with a body of water, you can use that as a place to do some sitting meditation, observing the changefulness of the water. Being mindful of how quickly things change helps you to become more accepting and flexible with other experiences in life.

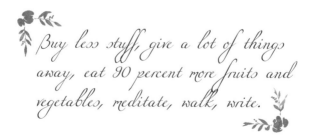

Buy less stuff, give a lot of things away, eat 90 percent more fruits and vegetables, meditate, walk, write.

Contemplate the way people exploit plants. Contemplate the many species lost every day, as through the destruction of the rain forest. Embrace all plants with your compassion. Wish for your compassion to ease their suffering.

Not living by the precepts is like living as a wild beast. You can be consumed by guilt, regret, self-hatred, and can do a lot of harm to others. When you're intoxicated by personal desires, there's no inner voice saying, *Wait a minute. Will what I am about to do cause harm to me or anyone else? Is there any benefit to what I'm about to do?*

At a time when troubled feelings threaten to blow you off course like a sailboat in a storm, sit in meditation and be aware of the storm. Watch the waves of negative feelings and thoughts as they wash over you. Accept their presence rather than try to avoid them. Observe the turbulence rather than identify with it. Move into the eye of the storm, into your center. Watch the storm die down and be replaced by a calm mind. Your boat will right itself and begin gliding again.

Objects of meditation can be natural: the breath, a burning candle, a plant. Creatively think of more!

Every morning before opening your eyes, stretch like a cat. After three or four minutes, begin to laugh. For five minutes, just laugh. Before long, laughing will be spontaneous and will change the nature of your whole day.

When life is hectic or stressed, remember that every hurricane has its eye, the still point in the middle of the raging winds. You too can retain a calm center, by remembering that your essential self is immune to circumstances. Trust in your ability to respond to any situation with the courage and wisdom you can draw from the core of your being.

Pick a time when you can look at the limitless, clear blue sky for at least five minutes. Then begin your meditation by closing your eyes. See each rigid expectation that you set for yourself as you would see yourself inviting a dark cloud, which limits your view of the possibilities. The more clouds you create in your own mind, the more ominous the future will seem—yet the clear blue sky is always there. Let go of your expectations and allow the wide horizon to open up.

Allow your flower garden to be picked or barter for picking privileges in a neighbor's organic garden.

Get ready to walk before the sun comes up. Begin walking toward the sun as you see its first rays of light. Receive the sun's energy as you walk. Thank the sun for all it gives you: energy, light, sustenance, and warmth.

The peacock is associated in the west with vanity, but in the east, it tends to be linked with compassion. That's because the eyes in the bird's tail symbolize compassion that is all-seeing, a magnificent empathy that notices every need. To be truly compassionate, you must be watchful. Look for telltale signs that indicate when and how you can help yourself and others.

Whatever your faith or mindset, meditating while you walk is a pleasant, easy way to expand your powers of concentration since the practice requires no accessories and no quiet room or special circumstance. You can focus on your breathing and count out your breaths while walking to work. Just break your steps down into slow, mindful movements, and breathe. You may repeat a favorite inspirational verse or affirmation. Notice how the ground rises up to meet your feet.

Seasons are part of the vast scenario, the greater dance of life going on. Honor this natural phenomenon.

134

No matter where you are right now, look up and out any window, or go stand in a doorway or step outside. Just watch, silently, what the world of nature is doing around you. Let go of all other thoughts, past and future.

The scriptures of various religions offer their wisdom in the form of countless insights. What are we to do with these? One answer is to treat these words of wisdom as seeds, which you need to plant in the fertile soil of the heart. There they will grow and create a divine garden within yourself. Here you can spend your happiest hours.

Place an apple on a plate and close your eyes. Set aside all thoughts and preconceptions. Open your eyes and see the fruit as if for the first time. Touch it and start to cut it, noticing every aspect. Raise a part slowly to your lips and pause. Open your mouth, bite down, and feel the texture of the flesh and the taste of its juice. Continue to bite and chew slowly, pausing between swallowing and biting again. Be aware of the sensations from moment to moment.

Attend to difficulties like they are struggling plants. Treat them with compassion and unconditional love.

In autumn, meditate on the bounty of nature's gifts. In spring, meditate on the new life that is blossoming. In summer, meditate on the bounty of green and sunlight. In winter, meditate on stillness, peace, and renewal.

Cats are the ultimate meditators. They sit absolutely still, being in the present moment for hours and hours. But if there is any movement or sound, the cat is immediately aware. The cat is there, undistracted by thoughts, resting in that state of awareness. It lives fully and joyfully in the moment. A cat can be a great teacher for you.

Do sky-gazing meditation. Relax into your posture. Be natural as a child dropping its body to the grass. Drop your mind. Let it rest in simplicity and awareness. Chant, *ah*. Raise your gaze. Elevate the scope of your awareness until it reaches a full 360 degrees. Be mindful, present. Rest in the natural state. Like a child lying in the grass watching the clouds roll by, allow everything to simply pass through the sky. Rest in that sky-like nature of mind. Enjoy the spectacle.

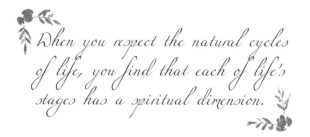

When you respect the natural cycles of life, you find that each of life's stages has a spiritual dimension.

Imagine the earth in your mind as a small blue-and-green planet orbiting the sun. Feel love and respect for this living thing on which you depend. Resolve to express these feelings through daily respect for the planet.

In July 1969, two men spent a day on the surface of the moon, then returned safely to earth. The computer used for this space mission was no bigger than the kind commonly used today in cars. The first moon landing was a tremendous feat of technology and courage. Next time you look at the moon, think of it as a stamp in the passport of civilization.

See yourself as a beautiful lotus flower, emerging strong and alive from the mud of materialism through the waters of experience toward the sunshine of enlightenment, where you blossom. Just as the lotus stands up in mud and water but has its own transcendent substance, the events and circumstance of your life that surround you are not part of your unique essence, so you need not identify yourself with them. Grow always toward the light.

If the roots hold firm, a felled tree grows up again. If desires are not uprooted, sorrows grow again in you.

As you get ready to leave your home, consciously approach the door. Take three slow, deep breaths. Do you have what you need? Walk out the door and enter the world with your eyes wide open and a smile on your face.

It is said that each time you catch a fall leaf as it drops from a tree, you win a wish for the coming year. And there are few more hilarious, live-in-the-moment activities than chasing leaves around on a golden autumn afternoon. Catching them is harder than you think, but each time you succeed, close your eyes and make your wish.

Light a soy or beeswax candle, turn off the lights, and sit at least two feet away, staring at the candle for minutes. When the mind wanders, note this and bring it back to totally paying attention to the flame. Become the flame. Blow out the candle and close your eyes. Watch the afterimage of the flame forming on the inside of your eyelids. Watch the flame. Go into the flame. Be flame. Let go and dissolve into the clear light in the natural mind. Meditate.

Show compassion toward animals and act on it. Donate to an animal charity or try to eat more vegetarian meals.

The rain replenishes and sustains, but it can feel inconvenient and even uncomfortable. Without deciding rain is good or bad, relax with the rain and feel whatever you are feeling. Choose to rain kindness on all.

When you are in the great outdoors, you put yourself in the midst of something greater than your personal difficulties, drama, and pain. The grandeur, openness, and space remove you from your narrow concerns and perspective. Rest at ease in a sense of open, expansive awareness, being open to nature and all that arises within it.

Do a mindfulness meditation centered on flower arranging, especially for spring. Choose the blossoms carefully. Look at each flower or piece of greenery. Get a feeling of where it was grown and how it blossomed. Cut off the bottom of each stem carefully, attentively, and lovingly. Find a container that suits the arrangement. Put water in the vase. Arrange the flowers one by one. Remain in the moment and do not rush. Place the flowers where they can be viewed.

Walking up a path or hill, use the feeling of effort in your thigh muscles lifting your body to become mindful.

Imagine entering the outer gates of a walled town. You walk through a labyrinth of narrow streets and eventually come to a peaceful green. Use this visualization when your journey through life seems difficult.

We all start adult life with an eagle and a dove inside us. The eagle is strong and decisive; the dove is peaceful and nurturing. As we grow in maturity, the two birds coalesce into one. You can act decisively with kindness, you can show strength and gentleness simultaneously. Keep your eagle compassionate and your dove fearless.

Breathe in through the nose and then out through the mouth. At the end of each exhale, pause, waiting patiently and consciously until the body initiates the next inhale. Every breath in is slow and calm through the nose. At the top of the inhale, release air through the open mouth slowly and calmly and then, with the mouth open and jaw relaxed, pause. Wait until the body chooses to inhale again. During each pause, allow your body to deeply relax and let go.

Recognize a thought's inherent emptiness. It will dissolve without a trace, like a bird flying through the sky.

Visualize diving into the water of a warm calm lake. It is silent in the water. You are in awe of the beauty of the lake bed. Return to the surface and feel the silence, purity, and beauty of this experience.

No one wants to impose their particular interests on friends, but it can be fun for both sides if you invite an unlikely friend along from time to time to share your hobby, such as visiting a nature reserve. You may gain fresh perspectives that make you value your pursuit more—or question it, which is no less rewarding.

Awareness can be helped by movement; being sedentary can often encourage daydreaming (unless you're meditating). Instead of taking the elevator, pretend you are climbing a mountain and walk up the stairs. Or instead of parking close to your destination, make a habit of parking farther away and walk outside to the place you are going. You might even choose to treat this as a meditative exercise, and silently repeat a mantra to yourself as you climb or walk.

Even when it rains, the sunshine is always there a little bit above the clouds. Find the sun behind the clouds.

Do object meditation. Concentrate on a particular object, feeling its presence and focusing on its texture, shape, or other qualities. A crystal, candle flame, flower, mandala, etc. are all suitable objects.

When you feel funny about taking time to meditate, think of bird migration and the rest stops they must make or else they get disoriented and off-course. Taking time each day to meditate helps you find a center from which you are able to deal with the changes and waves of daily life. You become more oriented and stay on your path.

Create a personal retreat. Draw up a program for the day with the number and length of your meditation sessions. Four twenty-to-thirty-minute sessions may be enough. Decide what you will do between sessions: read books on meditation, spend time outside, or do physical labor like clean or garden. Prepare your food beforehand, keeping it simple and frugal. Drink only water or juice. Enlist the cooperation of anyone who lives with you so that you can keep silent for the whole day.

Henry David Thoreau claimed he needed four hours a day of sauntering through the woods, free from worldly engagement. He understood the art of walking. He advised people to walk like a camel, which ruminates while slowly traveling. Walking is an accessible and easy form of meditation.

Close your eyes and imagine cleansing spring water pouring into you through the top of your head down through your feet. The water brings positive ions and washes out negative ions during meditation.

When your mouth offers only wisely chosen speech, you sow beautiful seeds in the garden of your heart and life.

Children are horrified when they see or hear of an animal suffering, yet some of us lose this sensitivity as we grow older. Reawaken your sense of compassion toward animals and act on it: this may mean donating to an animal charity, or turning vegetarian. Kindness toward all sentient beings is a tenet of most major religions.

When we think of unknown places, we think big. But an area of just a few square yards can be described as a place such as a patch of a wood or a public park. Find one of these small-scale places and get to know it thoroughly. Narrow your focus and look closely. There might be interesting insects or invertebrates or a fascinating fragment of litter. If there's nothing else, just look at the blades of grass; Walt Whitman wrote a great work of poetry on the subject.

Watch when the waves of negative feelings and thoughts wash over you. Accept their presence. Observe the turbulence. Move into the eye of the storm. Watch the storm die down and be replaced by a calm mind.

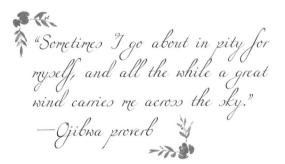

"Sometimes I go about in pity for myself, and all the while a great wind carries me across the sky."
—Ojibwa proverb

There's something strangely moving about the plum tree, which blossoms in late winter before its leaves appear, as if it were exceptionally eager to please. In the East its flowers symbolize strength triumphing over adversity. In late winter when you see plum trees blossom, enjoy the contrast of beautiful flowers against bare branches.

Explore having a beginner's mind. Work with an object in nature you know well or see very often. Stand or sit next to this object and take it in with all of your senses. After about five minutes, touch the object and start to explore it as you never have before. Involve all of your senses and experience the flow of time dropping away while you become your most curious self. You have no expectations. There is no right or wrong way to inhabit beginner's mind.

Watch a bird build its nest, a flower slowly open its petals, butterflies play tag, the grass grow, the moon rise.

Meditate on the sunset to help you understand endings and loss. When the sun sinks, surrender to the final moments of the day. Know that there will be a new day. Take strength from this process of renewal.

Why rush through some moments to get to other better ones? You do not have to fill up your moments with activity and more thinking in order for them to be rich—quite the opposite is true. Be completely open to each moment, accepting it in its fullness knowing that, like the butterfly, things unfold in their own time.

Do a movement meditation lying on the floor by an open window or a glass door that looks out on a natural scene. First breathe in and out and relax. Then, starting with the head, move your head in whatever way seems natural. Then bring it back to rest. Do this through each body part down to your toes. Move naturally this way and that. When you are ready to end this meditation, acknowledge and appreciate your efforts.

Look out a window and see how wondrous life is. Be attentive to each moment. Your mind is as clear as a calm river.

As you prepare to start your day, envision a large, happy lion stretching and roaring. Raise your arms and spread them wide, palms forward. Stretch. Breathe. Like the lion, leap forward into your day.

Become aware of the suffering caused by exploitation, social injustice, and oppression. Commit yourself to cultivate loving-kindness and learn ways to work for the well-being of people, animals, and plants. Commit to practice generosity by sharing your time, energy, and material resources with those who are in real need.

When you want to run instead of walk, to take dancing steps on and off the pavement, to bowl a hoop, to throw something up in the air and catch it again, or to stand still and laugh at nothing, do it! Turn the corner of your own street and be overcome by a feeling of bliss. Feel like you swallowed a bright piece of that late afternoon sun and it burned in your bosom, sending out a little shower of sparks into every particle, into every finger and toe.

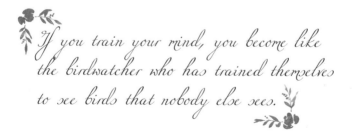

If you train your mind, you become like the birdwatcher who has trained themselves to see birds that nobody else sees.

Be like bamboo and bend with the wind. If bamboo were stiff, it would break. But because bamboo yields, it overcomes the wind. In the face of the strong wind, remain firm and steady as bamboo would.

Scientists believe that our emotional reaction to certain scents may be related to the close connection of the olfactory organs and our limbic system, which controls instinctive behavior. Capitalize on the power of scents by using evocative fragrance in your home. Buy fresh, sweet-scented flowers, herbs, and plants.

To learn something about our dependence on technology, and show that this is not the only way to live, avoid using electricity for a whole summer's day—an entertaining experiment for the weekend if you live with a partner or children, or want to try a solitary meditation. Rise with the dawn, savor each daylight hour, eat food unheated, read by candlelight, or maybe even go to bed at dusk. You'll find this an enlightening and perhaps a liberating experience.

By learning to recognize what to consume and what to reuse, you keep your mind and body healthy and preserve the earth.

Imagine that in front of you is a large open palm. Climb onto the cushioned palm and curl up. The hand closes in protection around you. The hand then rocks you and you feel loved, safe, and warm.

Planting a flower, shrub, or tree can be one of the best and simplest ways to help the planet. Choose a plant that is native to the area that may benefit the area in some way, or you may decide to plant a garden so you can grow your own fruit and/or vegetables or plant flowers that provide nectar for bees.

Sit outdoors comfortably with the legs crossed. Breathe through your nose and close your eyes. Inhale deeply through your nose, drawing breath into the belly. Hold your breath and visualize multicolored energy in your solar plexus, behind the stomach, spiraling inward. Exhale slowly through your nose and visualize a well of energy in your solar plexus from which you can draw nourishment for your body, mind, and spirit. Repeat this exercise three to five times.

See opinions forming and melting away like snowflakes. See that each comment is like a bubble, popping into nothingness.

On a cold day when you don't choose to go outside, take time to meditate by lying down in a warm room in a sunbeam or, if there is no sunlight that day, visualize the sun beating down upon you.

Bring the healing power of plants into your home and office. The most important places for your plants are the places where you spend the majority of your time. Some plants are particularly well suited to purify indoor air. Examples are bamboo palm, Boston fern, English ivy, gerbera daisy, and spider plants.

Harvesting is a time-honored activity, and one that is easy to participate in during the summer and fall. Harvesting results from a lot of hard work on nature's part. You can participate, being mindful of nature's effort. Find a local farm that offers fruit or vegetable picking and join in. Enjoy the textures, sights, and fragrances of the ripening year. Celebrate the culmination of the work that brings fruits and vegetables to be enjoyed by many.

Plant good roots today. Plant healthy seeds of joy, peace, and happiness and strengthen the healthy seeds already in you.

158

Bow gently. Close your eyes and imagine the Buddha garbed in warm yellow robes, sitting under the spreading bodhi tree. Visualize him in meditation, radiating peace and joy. Dissolve into that.

The fall colors are justly celebrated, and New England offers some of the best locations, scenic drives, optimum viewing dates, and so on. Find glorious leaf hues in fall and reflect on beauty that must always, and without regret, yield its place to the cycle of nature.

Visualize yourself at the base of a mountain whose summit is in a cloud. You start on this long, difficult journey, concentrating on the present moment and putting one foot in front of the other. You trust that the path will get you to the summit even though it is in the cloud. Near the summit, the clouds disperse and the way becomes clear. This meditation teaches that as long as you gather the strength to continue, you can conquer challenges.

Appreciate the diversity of beings you encounter. Like flowers, they bring beauty, variety, and sustenance to your world.

Move silently in nature. This takes practice. By walking as quietly as possible, you will glimpse a world that lies hidden to most. You will hear sounds that teach you the language of nature.

Fresh flowers are seldom inappropriate as a gesture of thanks—unless, of course, you need to thank someone for a gift of flowers! Ensure that your thank-you gesture doesn't dwarf the thing that prompted it. Moreover, it often feels right to choose something different in kind, as well as smaller in scale.

Meditate on an attachment you would like to be rid of, an addiction or dependence you have. Visualize yourself walking across a landscape toward a place you want to be. There is a rope tied to you and on the other end is a box carrying the attachment. You take a knife and cut the rope, making the conscious decision to let go of the attachment. This is a turning point. The rest of the walk is easier now that you have let go of the attachment.

It feels so much better to gently remove an insect or other pest from inside your home and put it outside than to kill it.

On a breezy day, as you walk, feel the wind's expression by the sounds it makes as it moves all around you and other objects. Do you detect a message that the wind has communicated to you?

Become more and more loving and you will become more and more joyful. It does not matter if it is a person, an animal, or a rock. Sit by a rock and have a chat. Stroke the rock and feel as one with it. The rock may not return anything, but that is not the point of love. You become joyful because you loved.

Take periods of silence and retreat regularly throughout the year for the renewal and deepening of practice. Either go on meditation retreats or take personal retreats alone at home or at a retreat center. Similarly, days of retreat and rest in nature such as hiking in the mountains or along the ocean, journeys of silence and listening, are all nurturing to practice. Silent time can renew your spirit and reconnect you with the simplicity of life.

Figure that your life is like a toy snow dome and meditating helps the flaky stuff settle down so you can see more clearly.

Go outside to take in some deep breaths. Trees and plants are involved in creating the air you breathe. Focus on your breathing and look deeply into it. Experience these connections fully.

Freshly squeezed fruit and vegetable juices are revitalizing and delicious: they contain little fiber, but their nutrients are speedily absorbed. Try mixing vegetables with fruits as part of your juicing routine. Carrot and orange is a classic combination; or try apple and beet, or celery and pomegranate.

Listen to the white sound of water. Enter into the contemplative space, the flow, the reflectiveness of water. Concentrate on the sound of water and let it wash everything else away. Let the sound wash over you, through you. Open your eyes, then look at the water. Let all thoughts fall into the water and dissolve. The waves come and go; watch until you forget yourself and become one with the waves. Be the sound; flow with the water.

Acting with virtue takes you toward the wind of enlightenment. Acting from virtue leads to virtue, which leads to happiness.

Mindfully explore your sense of touch. Feel the grass, the pavement, or sand at the beach. Feel rain or snow falling on you. Sense what the wind feels like on exposed parts of your body.

When you consume less of earth's natural resources and lessen your carbon footprint, even a single day each week, you give the planet a much-needed respite from humankind's constant demands. When you protect earth's environment, you begin to understand the intricate web of interrelatedness in the world.

Compose a haiku, preferably in a restful outdoor setting. Enter a calm meditative state of mind. Be aware of your surroundings and the atmosphere. Be aware and see what arises. A haiku usually has seventeen syllables, but you could start with eight to twelve words, no matter the number of syllables. Once you have written a haiku, do not try to improve it. Leave it as it is. Your haiku will present itself at the right time, like it has always existed.

A true practitioner of Dharma should be like a bee that is never attracted to just one flower, but flies from one to another.

Do an analytical meditation in the fall to contemplate the laws of karma in your own life. This kind of meditation is a way to gain greater awareness into the nature of reality.

Why is it that tombstones and gravestones with age, softened lettering, and maybe a patina of lichen, have something reassuring about them? Perhaps we feel that death, in old cemeteries, has been seasoned by nature, and thus lost some of its bite. Cemeteries are wonderful places to meditate or be at peace.

Close your eyes and imagine rowing down a river. You try to stay in the middle, but it is hard with the cross-currents. So, decide to let the boat drift instead of steering it. The boat is carried along with the current. You are free to enjoy the experience. When you come out of this meditation, take this attitude into daily life. Try to release the need to control things in life. Doing this will bring you a greater sense of peace.

A senses practice can be used for meditating in nature. Go through each of your senses and name five things you notice about each sense: five things you are seeing, smelling, tasting, feeling, and hearing.

Awareness that focuses entirely inward into the mind, the spirit, and the self while failing to give due attention to the wonders of nature and the universe, is merely a partial experience. To travel onward you need to go joyfully out into the world as well as deep into the recesses of your being.

Lie down in a comfortable position. Watch your breath. Imagine that you are simply a skeleton lying on the earth. Maintain a half-smile and keep following your breath. See the bones of each part of your body clearly. Scan the bones. See that your skeleton is not you, your bodily form is not you. You are one with the atmosphere, with your surroundings. You are everywhere and every moment. Continue this meditation for twenty to thirty minutes.

Investigation and contemplation can be done at any time: during meditation, while watching the ocean, or even while walking.

Touch! Close your eyes and touch anything in nature. Close your eyes and feel a communication from your heart to that entity.

Go on a gratitude walk. Look around and find the great, pleasing, beautiful, funny details in each thing. Feel the gratitude for all of these things over the twenty to thirty minutes of the walk.

A brief excursion in a hot air balloon is a popular adventure these days. Take advantage of this opportunity when an excursion is offered. Entering the unfamiliar element of air and seeing the landscape from a bird's-eye perspective healthily undermines our habitual modes of perception—and the views can be exhilarating!

Go into the woods and spend five minutes looking at the trees. Then close your eyes or shut them a little and visualize yourself as a tree with branches reaching to the sky and roots extending into the earth. On alternate inhalations, draw air and sunlight in and exhale them down into your roots. On the other inhalations, imagine gathering energy from the earth up through your roots and exhale this energy through your branches.

Right underneath your thoughts and negative emotions exists an ocean of love. One simply has to quiet the mind to experience it.

If someone apologizes to you, accept their apology gracefully. It is like appreciating the sunshine after the rain, putting down that umbrella.

During the warmer months, commit to one week during which you will not kill any bug. Become aware of your emotions, frustrations, and desire to kill. What happens when you do not kill?

The Sanskrit word *karma* simply means "action" or being sensitive to the results of your own actions. Every action ripples through the community of souls; its effects are more or less widespread depending on the nature of each action. Make efforts to ensure that your ripples will have positive effects when they make landfall.

Do a visualization meditation. Imagine yourself and your body as a clear ball of light, a crystal clear and luminous sphere of white light and pure being. Envision a golden sun at the heart center, opening like a sunflower. Warm and illuminate all who wander through the darkness of ignorance and delusion. Awaken spiritual awareness and joy like the dawn. Let go and see the afterglow. Simply be in the joy and peace of this meditation.

Ride the events of life. You cannot tame the laws of nature or change. Just stay in the saddle when the horse becomes unruly.

Practice loving-kindness (metta) on nature and natural objects. Say to each object, "May you be free from danger. May you have physical happiness. May you have ease of well-being. May you have peace."

Inspire yourself: Make a couple of small changes so that you feel the benefits of invigorated habits. Eat a meal in an unusual place in your home, take dinner outside, eat lunch on your porch, or sit on the floor for breakfast. At one of these meals, include a fruit or vegetable you've never tried.

You can attune yourself to the cycle of the seasons by making a flower arrangement on the Zen principle of three (heaven, earth, human world). Cut a Y-shaped fork from pliable wood and wedge it horizontally an inch down in the mouth of a flower vase to provide support. Place each flower into the vase, being very careful to keep the arrangement open and not obscure any flowers. The act of flower arranging is a meditation in itself.

Do a thank-you prayer for the gift of sight, the gift of hearing, the gift of smell, the gift of taste, and the gift of touch.

Walk next to a body of water that is flowing, a brook, river, stream, or lake. Close your eyes and pause to listen to the water. Then open your eyes and observe its fluidity. Notice how water is also flowing through your body as part of the action of arteries, veins, and organs. Commit to becoming more fluid yourself in how you deal with obstacles and changes. Carry water's lessons with you into your day.

Thousands of snowflakes have piled up. Mindfully, gather them onto a shovel and place them aside, clearing a path. Your path is mindfulness. On this beautiful path, walk in peace.

Be grateful and do not take for granted that you are able to fill your bowl when so many in this world cannot. Next time you eat a meal, show appreciation to those who work out of sight to plant, raise, harvest, and prepare the food for your comfort. Remember them and be grateful for them.

Breathe in the lessons that green things teach you about cycles of the seasons, life and death, and the unity of the elements.

Sit or stand in a peaceful outdoor space. Know that you are breathing in. Know that you are breathing out. Ask yourself if your thought, feeling, or perception is creating suffering or well-being. Explore the contents of your thought, feeling, or perception. Allow its true nature to be revealed. Ask who created this. Answer and smile. Ask if this thought, feeling, or perception is who you are. Answer and smile. Dwell in the present moment.

Think of your loved ones as a garden. Gather your loved ones in your mind and care for them. Think of helping them grow and blossom as you would tend to garden plants and flowers.

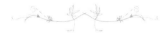

Appreciate weather forms. Many are beautiful: snow, sunshine, dawn mist, even rain. Don't get into the habit of treating every day's weather as an irrelevance or a nuisance. We live among the weather of our world and our emotions, and if we are mindful of both, our lives will be enriched.

If you hurt an innocent person, then you are only hurting yourself, just as dust thrown into the wind is blown back in your face.

If worry forms a background buzz to your thoughts and fills your mind whenever you're not actively concentrating, it may have become habitual. Sit somewhere quiet and visualize a green layer of algae sitting atop the surface of a pond. Imagine taking a large scoop and skimming the algae off the water's surface. Gradually the pond becomes clear again. You've discarded all those niggling concerns. You feel pure, light, and focused.

Whatever the day's weather, you must accept it. To complain about the rain or lack of it shows a mind out of tune with nature.

Picture yourself sitting on the bank of a gentle river and, from time to time, see a log come floating down the river. Follow the log, observing it floating past and out of sight.

Fractals are particular shapes that are found in mathematics and certain natural organisms, repeated over and over at increasingly smaller scales. Find an example of a fractal in nature like a snowflake or a fern. Contemplate how the tiniest part of the pattern is a minute expression of the whole.

Before you walk, tell the earth that you are glad to be with her and ask for help in healing your wounds. As you walk, feel the enormous energy of the earth beneath your feet. Tell the earth about your challenges and problems. When you are done talking, draw in the earth's energy with your breath. Let negative thoughts float to the top of your head and float away. The earth's healing energy has filled you up.

Happiness comes when your work and words benefit both yourself and others. Karma says if you plant peaches, you will get peaches.

Taking off your shoes changes how you experience things. Walk slowly, paying attention to each new sensation on bare feet. Challenge yourself with different terrains or surfaces.

When you meditate with your eyes open, you can begin to notice how your environment affects your inner experience. This can help you feel connected to the world around you, as it becomes clear that you are in fact part of the environment you are inhabiting, rather than separate from it.

Resting in water is an easy way to heal and return to your natural state. Relax in a bathtub, hot tub, Jacuzzi, pool, or preferably a pond, lake, or calm ocean. Let your tension drain away. Be open and vulnerable. Drop your cares. Rest, relax, breathe slowly. Let it all go. Melt into the water. Watch your mental events and experiences like clouds. Rest in wholeness and completeness, simplicity and buoyancy.

When performing a chore like clearing the snow, try focusing all of your attention on your hands. Note the sensations. If a thought comes, let it go and refocus on your hands.

Take a more personal approach to nature: get to know the names and traits of individual trees, flowers, insects, or birds as if they were personal friends. Allow this approach to involve you more intimately in the profound beauty and relaxing rhythms of the natural world.

Every time you think of helping someone else become more generous and giving, you plant very powerful seeds within your own mind.

Five things to contemplate before eating: 1) This food is the gift of the whole universe: the earth, the sky, and much hard work. 2) Be aware of the quality of your deeds as you receive the food. 3) Practice mindfulness to transform greed, hatred, and ignorance. 4) Ask that the food nourish you and prevent illness. 5) In gratitude, accept the food so you may realize the path of love, compassion, and peace.

Nature shows that you cannot hold back the tide or make the seasons turn faster. Each season changes and changes in its own time.

Imagine that you are a single drop of water in the sea. Together with billions of other drops, you form an ocean. Meditate upon your spirit, one among many, but part of One.

Closing the door to honest feedback from others is like cutting the string on a kite that is flying free in the wind. Your mind drifts farther from the ground of reality and you are tossed around by the winds of fear. Listen and do not add your own judgment or ideas to what others say.

Ask nature and the universe for help when you feel trapped, stuck, or at your wit's end. Step out of your mind and your attempts to think a problem into submitting a solution. Ask a favorite rock or tree or your plot of flowers for some wisdom. It may seem silly at first, but you may very well be surprised at the result of getting out of your head and letting the larger world suggest a path for you to try.

Running is the fastest form of unaided locomotion available to humankind, apart from falling. To be able to run for a mile or more is a skill you should value and exercise if you can. Fight gravity and inertia; allow your lungs and legs to show their courage. After a good run, lie on the ground and look up at the sky; you will feel connected to the earth and conscious of the privilege of being.

Take a day trip to explore the areas of historical interest or outstanding natural beauty near your home. You'll return refreshed.

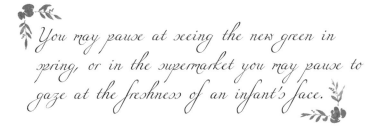

You may pause at seeing the new green in spring, or in the supermarket you may pause to gaze at the freshness of an infant's face.

Honor the life-giving power of the sun: stay up all night to watch the sunrise on the longest day of the year (June 21 in the northern hemisphere). Celebrate with a great breakfast.

Happiness is a universal phenomenon. Trees and animals and birds and plants are happy. The whole of existence is happy except for man. Being miserable is very specific to man. Misery makes you special but there is nothing special about happiness because it is a universal phenomenon.

Cultivate your garden with this meditation. Stand in a garden. Breathe in the air, the fragrances, the light, the temperature, the music of the plant and animal life in the garden. Breathe out through your mouth the carbon dioxide that helps sustain the plants. Inhale the energy of these growing things. Feel nature enter you with every breath in. Do this for fifteen to twenty minutes.

Take moments for short meditations, affirmations, and offerings to appreciate all that you have. Light a candle, watch nature, hug somebody.

Imagine yourself building a snowman. Off-load all your stress and resentments to him, then imagine the sun melting the snowman along with all those negative feelings.

Do you have the patience to wait until your mind settles before you act? Frustrations with people or situations are occasions to practice patience, letting your mind settle before taking action.

A global awareness meditation: sit quietly and contemplate all the things that are going on around the earth right now. Let your thoughts calm into a deep awareness of where you are. Offer blessings or a prayer to the world. Become gently aware of the different emotions and physical and mental states of everyone out there, including animals and plants. Realize that all of it is a play of the divine.

The teacher's pointing finger isn't the moon. Don't look at your teacher to give you the answers. Look where the finger is pointing.

During the day, whenever something ruffles or disturbs you, recall an image of a mountain lake. Feel its ripples and the coolness of the ripples, then feel them settle.

Encourage children you know to explore the beauty of nature. Show them different features such as buds, caterpillars, lichen, or ants' nests, and explain how one life-form relates to another. Then get the kids to write poems about what they've seen, perhaps in brief, haiku form.

Simply planting a seed with the intention of connecting with the earth can be transformative. In the garden, notice the earth, feel the soil, smell the air. Be fully present to the act of planting and the sensation of touching soil. State your intention to the seed, aloud or silently, "May you grow and may you be healthy." Plant the seed gently and water lightly. Breathe.

Experience your feelings without resistance, let them go, and move forward. Emotions come and go like an ocean wave.

Listen to the sounds of silence, within which you may find the wind murmuring, leaves rustling, birds flapping their wings, swallowing in your throat, and your quiet breathing.

The mind is like a creeper plant that needs support to help it grow healthily with purpose; without this support, it may wander aimlessly or out of control. Indian philosophy teaches us to cultivate self-support in the form of spiritual exploration, dedication, and discipline.

Be like a lotus flower opening its heart to drink the morning sun. Be the center of a thousand-petaled lotus flower, thinking of a center word associated with good feelings for you such as home, light, love, or peace. Sitting, let the word come to you. Follow the path of this word to another word your mind associates with it. Stay there for a few seconds, then return to the center word and wait for the next word association.

Refrain from mindless consumption and forgo using products and services that unduly harm animals, plants, humans, and non-sentient life.

Imagine that you are a kite soaring high in the sky. Revel in your surrender to the wind but be aware of the string that anchors you to the ground and keeps you safe.

As the sun sets each day, notice the quality of the sky as it moves from afternoon to night. The dusk can be as lovely as the dawn in its own understated way. As the sun sets, practice awareness. Appreciate the numerous beings who offered guidance and support along your path today.

Energy storms come and go in the mind, stirring up restlessness. Acknowledge this and breathe long, slow, deliberate breaths. Relaxed breathing calms the body and settles the mind. Energy levels change in the mind just as they do in the body. Acknowledge your energy state, whatever it is. Keep your eyes open. Try to aim the mind precisely by noting the beginning and ending of each breath.

It would be easier not to go to all the trouble of constantly ruminating over your suffering. It would be better just to sit in nature.

A technique for going-to-sleep meditation is to imagine that with each breath you become filled with more light and space. Melt into an ocean of light and space.

When you contemplate the future, its lack of known features is often the thing that makes you apprehensive. You may not know what's going to happen, but you can be sure that many things will. Think of the future as a garden you have planted, but have not yet seen bloom.

Choose a place to sleep outside, like a tent or screened-in porch. As you prepare to fall asleep, take in all the noise you hear at night that you do not hear in the daytime. Focus on the individual sounds instead of on your breath for this meditation. At some point, you will start thinking, making your own internal noises. When you recognize that, bring yourself back to attentive listening.

Meditate in nature as often as you can, taking note of your state of mind and heart. Concentrate on your breath or the sounds of nature.

When you arrive home from work, acknowledge that you have arrived at home in the here and now. You are free to proceed in peace. With each action, a lotus blooms.

Fire yoga poses produce heat and light in different areas of the body. Fire poses aid digestion and clears energy blocks. Examples of fire yoga poses are boat pose, shoulder stand variations, and twists. All of these can be done on the grass or on a mat in a park or clearing in the woods.

A meditation for the root chakra: Sit quietly, close your eyes, and take a few slow deep breaths, relaxing. Rest your awareness gently on your behind. Take the first image that comes and sit with it. Ask what the chakra would say if it could speak. Ask what animal the chakra would be. You may not feel a response to one of these inquiries. It is okay, you are simply touring the chakra.

No matter how hectic or troublesome things appear, you need only to turn inward to find peace. In the eye of a storm there is stillness.

193

Imagine wading into a clear, cool river and feeling its power coursing through your body. Sense the river as a source of inner strength, running deep inside of you.

Consider a tropical fish in an aquarium: he believes that the ocean is a ten-second swim from one glassy rock-face to another. We're all conditioned by our circumstances to believe that our lives are typical. Let your imagination rove, and find new possibilities for yourself.

Imagine that the way you walk during your walking period is the way you will be walking through all of eternity. This will encourage you to choose the way you will be walking through eternity by walking that way now. During the first part of the walk, bring to mind all the things you need to change. In the second part of the walk, start making positive statements about the changes.

Time spent in nature is healing. It can ground you and reaffirm your connection with the world. Spend time in nature as often as you can.

Visualize your desires as a group of wild horses dragging you in a cart. Take the reins and gently but firmly tighten them, slowing the horses and gaining control.

Become aware of any living beings in your world (people, animals, plants) you ignore or take for granted, and cultivate a sense of reverence for them. This deep respect is important. When you have a deep respect for others, you also have a deep respect for yourself.

A cold shower meditation is a good way to practice softening to an uncomfortable feeling. Make the water a bit colder than you normally prefer. Clear your mind and be compassionate. Push your limits but without being self-punishing. (This could also be done with hotter-than-normal water.) Gradually change the shower setting and see how long you can stay centered and focused.

In divided times, bees can teach us to live in a harmonious society where individuals live for the benefit of the whole group or society.

Try the thousand-petal lotus meditation: All things, by immortal power, near and far, are linked to each other. You cannot stir a flower without troubling a star.

Try to teach your children that they are free in each moment to shape not only their own lives but also the world. What they plant, they will reap. If they can sacrifice a little and conserve water and other natural resources, this action will benefit them and all others.

Of all sensations to savor, silence can be the most satisfying. There's no better way to beat stress than a totally silent meditation. Even finer for many is the silence over which lovely, gentle sounds drift: clinking cowbells, birdsong, or a distant stream. Find a place of silence and one by one tune in to the sounds of earth and sky. Let stress be busy elsewhere.

Prepare for sitting in meditation with one or more yoga poses: cat/cow, cobra, locust, lunge/pigeon, butterfly, cradle, or sun salutation.

Go to the quietest place you know. Sit and let your mind and body settle. Let everything in this setting fade until you are left with an emptied mind.

Surfers say that the ocean is their greatest teacher. Like the ocean, awareness will throw surprises our way: swirling undercurrents, peaks, and troughs. Be courageous—and patient. Mastery and balanced equilibrium will come if you're willing to learn this new skill.

You can create a sacred circle in your own backyard or in a natural setting that you like to frequent. Try to make the circle on a flat area with enough room for you to lie down in it. Use a compass to mark the four directions and then place an object at each of those points as well as one in the center. The central object is the Tao, the divine within the sacred circle.

Loving-kindness as a divine abode is often described as the sun whose rays shine indiscriminately on the whole earth and all living things.

Meditate on the full moon. The full moon is a time for gathering strength. Let its whiteness fill your consciousness and flood you with strength and energy.

Don't hide indoors. Appreciate the extremes of inclement weather just as you would a perfect sunny day. Wrap up warmly and enjoy the freezing air on your face. Splash through rainy puddles. You'll feel exhilarated, and all the more appreciative of your warm, dry home.

Next time you are in a park or on a beach, practice walking meditation. Walk slowly and deliberately, bringing complete attention to the placement of your feet—heel, ball of foot, toe—and how you transfer your weight on each step. Adopt the traditional hand gesture if you wish: make your right hand into a fist (thumb inside) and grasp this fist with your other hand.

Judge a tree by its fruits. You can always tell who someone is by the circumstances in which they grow. Never go shopping for kiwis in a shoe store.

Solve a problem by walking. Take a walk in a natural setting and focus on your footsteps. A walk can give you a new perspective on something that is puzzling you.

Be brave. Sample some regional dishes while you're abroad, no matter how unfamiliar the ingredients may seem. They'll often be fresh, seasonal, and prepared with pride—and they may even have hidden health benefits. Try fruits and vegetables not native to your area.

Do a sun breath practice before meditation. Stand in mountain pose with your hands by your sides. Breathe into your belly while stretching your arms. Breathe in and bring your hands to Namaste or prayer position at your heart. Stretch your hands out and exhale, then inhale, lifting your hands over your head. Exhale and lower your hands to your sides. Do this practice nine times.

Remember that as soon as you wash your car, it rains. Letting go of your attachment to a continuously clean car is a way to reduce suffering.

Your karma, like fruit, ripens from thoughts and actions you have planted. You do not know when it will manifest, but each thought and action will manifest someday. Be mindful of what you do in the moment to sow karmic seeds of happiness for yourself and the world.

See yourself as a surfer preparing to ride a big wave. You paddle out, see the wave coming, and get on your board. As the water comes up beneath you, you sense the wave's momentum and align the surfboard with the wave's direction. You ride the wave, visualizing yourself arriving safely on the beach. This visualization may help you ride the big waves of life.

Turn on the water faucet and imagine the water flowing down from the glaciers and mountains. See the water running deep in the earth, sustaining you and all life.

If you embrace a natural way of living, even a single day each week, you give the planet a much-needed sabbatical from your constant demands.

The ear is a door; it allows. It cannot do anything to existence; it can only let it happen. Listening to the birds, the wind, the rain, animals, the ocean—just listening, doing nothing—great silence comes in and great peace starts falling and showering on you.

As you prepare food using as many natural, organic ingredients as you can, acknowledge that the earth, water, sun, and air all live in the food you prepare.

Follow the practice of wu wei or non-interference with nature. Live in a state of simply being rather than constantly doing and achieving. Living with respect for nature is the best way to practice this. Observe weather patterns and seasonal changes. Value the wisdom of trees, the strength of the wind, the majesty of mountains, and the serenity of flowing water.

Make a relaxation tape using the gentle, relaxing sounds of nature. It should last at least ten minutes and be associated with pleasant memories.

205

On the telephone, make certain that your words create mutual understanding and love. Aim to have those words be as beautiful as flowers and gemstones.

Earth, water, sun, and air all live in the food you prepare. Feel gratitude for your food and all those beings involved in bringing it to your table. Prepare the meal with love and compassion, knowing that these feelings will nourish those you are feeding.

Protecting nature on a daily basis involves how individuals make choices versus just following a set of rules. By basing your actions on generosity, responsibility, wisdom, and respect, you can provide nature the protection she needs in order to flourish.

Visualize a lotus flower floating on a still, reflective pond. Imagine that it's filled with light radiating out from its green leaves from each separate, glowing petal, and from the bright center. Now imagine that the flower is blooming in your heart. The lotus is a potent symbol for the spirit: use this quick meditation whenever you need calm and balance.

It is best to use language only when it is useful to do so. To talk a lot unnecessarily is like allowing thousands of weeds to grow in a garden.

Cultivate the energy of mindfulness with mindful breathing and walking. Use these simple everyday acts to calm your emotions and nourish your joy.

Think of an activity that you associate with being calm, like lying in the sun or swimming in a pond. When you feel under pressure, think about such a relaxing activity. Your mind will associate this with peace and you will soon start to feel relaxed.

Pretend you are a predator when you walk in the woods so that you notice everything that moves and breathes as well as every color, pattern, and shape. Feel with all your senses and avoid being heard or seen by your "prey." Halfway through your walk, switch to being the prey. This practice will help you understand what most wildlife experience every day.

We don't realize all that the caterpillar goes through in order to become a butterfly. We don't realize the long and difficult transformation required.

Use your breath as the string that will guide you through the labyrinth in the garden or the bread crumbs that will lead you through the forest.

We have all had moments when the setting sun is simply a brilliance of orange and red and gold, when the grass is really green, or the sky is blue. When one is present in this way, the familiar seems quite unfamiliar, because everything seems so new.

Find a group of people to do Sufi movement meditation in which a circle is formed by clasping hands. Slowly lean backward with your faces to the sky and hands up and say "Ya hai." Bring bodies and heads forward and swing arms down and back and say "Ya huk." This is repeated until the speed and rhythm are coordinated and the circle opens and closes like a flower.

Earth and sky joined to create each flower. Each flower's beauty is a gift. When you see a flower, look deeply into the present moment and smile.

When you flush the toilet, acknowledge that your body's waste is returning to the earth to become compost. When nature calls, listen to Nature.

Read a book set in the area you'll be visiting before you go, perhaps by a local author. This could be a novel or a book about history, nature, or politics, whatever most interests you. Try to make connections between what you read and what you see or hear once you arrive at your destination.

Feel the forest, its age, general well-being, its mood, the feeling of community. Notice the trees living in harmony and the visitors coming and going. Observe all the life cycles of nature and the balance and harmony in the forest community. Listen to whatever the forest wants to teach you.

Walk on the edge of a beach where the water meets the sand. With your eyes closed, feel your way along, totally vigilant and attentive.

Whichever seeds you water will blossom and grow into plants. If you repeatedly act out of anger, you are watering the seeds of anger. If you meet your anger with kindness, the anger seeds cannot grow, but a loving plant will come in its place.

If you've truly loved reading a particular book, why not leave a copy somewhere public, like on a park bench, for a stranger to pick up and enjoy?

Speak this to yourself: A forest without monkeys. Although the forest has no monkeys, it's almost impossible not to imagine them—the very word "monkeys" summons them in your imagination. When you can imagine a forest truly without monkeys, you'll have become enlightened. Forget about the monkeys and let the forest rise in your being as love and peace.

Meditate on a pebble. Imagine you are a pebble sinking in a lake, effortless and detached, finally reaching the bottom and perfect rest.

Water flows, it never fights. It is flexible yet persistent enough to wear down rocks and carve out continents. Hear the sound of water gently falling into a glass as a soothing lullaby. Water helps bring your awareness to exactly where you are.

Those whose compulsions are gone, who are not attached to food, whose sphere is empty of negative thoughts, are hard to track, like birds in the sky.

Imagine sitting beneath a rainbow and gradually it expands through your body and dissolves all obstacles. Your body shines like a lamp and light streams in all directions, filling space. It dissolves the suffering of beings everywhere and the world now shines with great meaning and joy. Emanate this light as long as it feels natural.

Water yoga poses enable flow, flexibility, and balance. Water poses include legs on the wall, seal, bow pose, reclined twist, fish pose, and cobra.

If you have kids, take them outside and sit in a spot where you can keep them in your awareness. Take the time to breathe in a little peace.

The miracle is that the honey is always here, right under your nose, only you were too busy searching elsewhere to realize it. The worst is not death but being blind, blind to the fact that everything about life is in the nature of the miraculous.

Meditate on the profound power of the four elements—air, earth, fire, and water—and the enormity of their force. Give thanks for all that the elements offer us. Air is connected with purity and life-force. Earth is associated with nourishing energy. Fire is connected with passion and purification. Water is associated with cleansing and life sustainment.

Visit the trees and gardens around your house. Walk through the woods. Learn to name the flowers and plants. Take time to sit and reflect on nature.

Meditate and visualize yourself in an overgrown garden. You work in the garden to clear out the weeds and create something beautiful.

Capable of practicing silence, you are free as a bird, in touch with the essence of things. Sometimes you have to practice silence. Silence is a time for looking deeply. There are times when silence is truth, and that is called thundering silence.

Do a prayer meditation at night in a darkened room, going to sleep immediately afterward. Raise your hands toward the sky, palms up, head up. Feel energy flowing into your arms and then to your body. You will feel one with the earth. Then bend and touch the earth. Repeat this six more times so each of the chakras can become unblocked. Then go to sleep.

Animals have karma because they have consciousness and intention, but only humans can mindfully discriminate between wholesome and unwholesome acts.

Look at an image of the aurora borealis, the northern lights. Meditate on these shimmering sacred lights falling across the night sky.

We are not separate from plants and animals. Defend all of them as you would your own life. Recognize that you are part of the interconnected biosphere. Do what you can to protect an endangered species as you would care for a person who was ill.

Take a moment to be mindful of the change from summer to fall. Step outside on a fall day. Notice the quality of the light. Feel the air against your skin, cooler than it was just a few weeks ago. Observe the sunlight filtering through the trees. Notice the play of the shadows. Listen to the sounds of rustling leaves. Inhale the smell of an autumn day.

Become a large gray rock in your mind. Feel what it is like to be the rock. Feel the stillness. What lessons does the rock have to teach you?

The way in which a cut heals is explained by biology, but it remains an everyday marvel. Look at your hands, flex your fingers, and reflect on the mysterious processes that convert thought to action. You can't deny nature's miraculous character.

Contemplate the suffering of farm animals, the suffering of animals killed for sport, the suffering of animals bred for their fur, the suffering of animals used in experiments. Contemplate the suffering of animals due to the loss of their natural habitat. Embrace all animals with your compassion. Wish for your compassion to ease their suffering.

Keep potted plants, small shrubs, or climbing plants on trellises if you have space. They help keep the air clean and boost your spirit.

Convert taking out the trash into a walking meditation. Even a short walk, when done slowly and mindfully, can be a meditation.

Start being conscious of more objects in nature. Look at things with more alertness. You see a tree. Look at it with more alertness. Stop for a while. Collect your awareness. Suddenly, when you are alert, you may perceive the tree in a different light.

Live your life like a competent captain, setting a course and steering your boat when necessary, letting the wind and waves do most of the work.

Find your own way to commemorate those you have lost. A gift of flowers left in a churchyard or crematorium may seem arbitrary and small, but it gives you time, on the way there perhaps, to meditate on that person and be grateful for having known them and enjoyed their special gifts. You might prefer to leave flowers in a favorite spot instead.

Sitting in meditation is like sitting under the Bodhi tree. Your body is mindfulness itself, entirely free from distraction.

The earth brings us life and nourishes us, then swallows up nutrients and starts all over. As you work in the yard and the garden, see the birth and death in the earth's processes. Breathe and work with the earth. Prune the garden of your mind.

As you look through the fruits and vegetables at the market, recognize that they bear the blessings of life and that all things have a divine radiance.

When you need to reconnect with yourself, take a journey to somewhere rich in meaning for you, a place in nature, or a vantage point over land or sea. Think of the journey as a meditation. On arrival, settle down to at least twenty minutes of quiet reflection, drawing energy from the depths of your being and from the atmosphere of the place itself.

Think of your ego as a wild monkey that has gotten loose in the house of your mind. Shouldn't you put him back in the jungle before he does any damage?

Next time you look at the moon and stars through a telescope, think of the genius Galileo, for whom the night sky was an adventure, full of potential discoveries. Learn to recognize the most prominent planets, constellations, and star clusters.

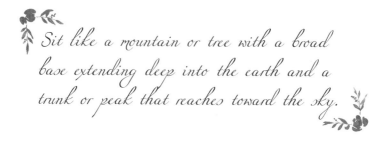

Sit like a mountain or tree with a broad base extending deep into the earth and a trunk or peak that reaches toward the sky.

Take a few moments to tune into the sounds around you and pause. Notice the sensation of air on your face and pause. Bring your awareness down into your feet and pause. Really feel the connection your feet are making with the earth beneath you. Realize that there is nowhere else you need to be at this moment. Take the time to connect with nature.

Remember you cannot step twice in the same river and you never meet the same person twice. Nothing remains the same; nature is the best teacher for this.

When you are meditating in nature, try to drop below the ordinary level of observation and be there with no agenda or expectations or judgment. Be part of the ecosystem, in relationship to all the life forms, participating in the aliveness.

Visualize a favorite outdoor place until you are one with nature and are transported to that beautiful spot in your mind.

Use an image of a lake and all the ways it changes in your meditation. See the times of stillness. See the times when it reflects. See the times of turbulence, even though it is calm beneath the surface. Use this image in daily life to carry you in difficult times.

Pick a peaceful place and do a mindful painting practice outside. Let nature's influence guide your brush on the canvas.

If you were enduring a long dark night of the soul, look for nature to be your main consolation. Understand that nature can comfort you in hard times, and you'll avoid the pitfall of taking it for granted when you're contented and at peace.

Appreciate a cardinal's brilliance against the snow, the fragrance of a summer rose, the last glow of the fireplace, the gentle sounds of a spring Sunday.

The healing mantra *Ra Ma Da Sa, Sa Say So Hung* translates to sun, moon, earth, infinity—I am Thou. Sit and bend the elbows with the palms of the hands facing upward and flat. Close your eyes and focus on the space between the eyebrows. Repeat this mantra once on each breath. Continue for five to thirty minutes. Relax for a few minutes when you are done.

Study the art of artists for whom nature is their inspiration, such as Ansel Adams, Georgia O'Keefe, and Monet. Do they inspire you to make art from nature?

Get into the habit of eating plenty of fresh fruit and vegetables every day. They contribute to our well-being by boosting the immune system, while at the same time providing us with a living connection with the vital energy of the earth.

Do a walking meditation with great attention to the feet as they leave the ground, move, and then touch the ground again.

Let yourself be drawn to something in nature that exemplifies peace. Sit for a while with it, your eyes open, taking in its peacefulness. Let your worries go and, instead, enter into calm. Your mind may become uneasy with this unusual stillness. Allow the peaceful object of your meditation to soothe you and teach you how to find your own peace.

You can appreciate nature through windows and screens, but in order to truly awaken, you need to get outside and be in nature. It's just outside your door.

Take a sound walk, where you focus on what you hear. Find a place to stop and listen to sounds with your eyes closed.

Nature is ready to help anyone who opens themselves to the gifts that she has to bring. All you have to do is open yourself to receive help and be present for what nature gives. The healing power of Nature can engulf your being.

Find a situation that is troubling you and which you have been trying to work out. Think about it and do nothing. Stop all unnecessary activity and thoughts. Take a walk and enjoy the moment. Keep walking and keep enjoying the moment. After about a week of this, note the changes that have taken place without your doing anything at all about it.

We are all caught up in the details of our lives when very little of it (or none of it) is worth a whole lot of energy. To relish, even rejoice in being alive, with the recognition that this life on earth is limited and will end—that is Zen.

Meditate on hair, which is ever-changing, a microcosm of nature's great cycles being played out on top of your head.

Try a spring Chi Kung exercise: Bring your palms to your heart and stretch them out to the sides slowly and purposefully. The spring energy is there within you, so that you start the day with a spring of energy inside you. Be like a budding seed opening its seedling case into two halves and stretching to make way for the new to spring upward.

Lie down on the grass and embrace the earth. Appreciate its support. Feel its energy and vibrations. Love the earth.

Mark off a one-foot or three-foot square of your yard with string and four sticks. Make an account of what is within the square. Then return each week and note what is new and changed. This is a great practice for observance.

Know that when you are raking, weeding, or pruning the garden, you are on a spiritual path to sense the pulse and sacred essence of man, nature, and objects.

Imagine yourself at the entrance to a maze, deciding which way to go. With every turn you take, think of a delusion falling from you. As you walk, you see only the walls of corn, bushes, or hay, yet there's a pattern as yet unseen. Once you reach the heart of the maze, you suddenly perceive this pattern from above, in a flash of recognition.

Health experts recommend that each of us walks ten thousand steps per day. Buy a pedometer and see how often you can hit this target, as much outside as possible.

Living Zen means to open yourself to a full awareness of your surroundings and yourself. You can use the storms, winds, and waves to propel you through life. You must lose yourself and become one with the water and wind.

Letting go of thoughts at the end of the out-breath is like moving a large rock away so that water can keep flowing.

Here is a mindfulness training: Aware of the suffering caused by the destruction of life, commit to cultivating compassion and learning ways to protect the lives of people, animals, plants, and minerals. Be determined not to kill, not to let others kill, and not to condone any act of killing in the world, in your thinking and your way of life.

Adopting a Zen attitude is like installing a new navigation system in your ship. The system is designed to work with the ocean and its many and varied waves.

Letting yourself be blown about by the winds of your negativities indicates that you have a completely misguided approach to life. Instead, you should savor the lasting delight that arises from skillful behavior and meditation.

When you walk, take a moment to consider what is underfoot and walk as if you are kissing the earth with your feet.

You can send healing intentions toward the earth or toward specific people, animals or plants. Sit in meditation and feel yourself filled with warm energy. Visualize the earth, the people, animals, or plants, and then send positive energy to that focus. Let your energy flow out and fill the focus and imagine it renewing and healing the earth, people, animals, or plants.

Cozy up in a secluded private spot outdoors. The idea is that you are taking good care of yourself and are in nature.

One of the five daily duties performed by Hindus is giving food and water to anyone or anything in need. Next time you are watering a withering plant or putting food out for winter birds, think of these actions in this light.

Going outside for some fresh air, taking a walk in a park, or hiking deep into the woods heightens your attention and brings you immediately into the present.

Consciously engage your sense of sight. Start by turning slowly and deliberately, taking a 360-degree view. Look up, explore the sky, the patterns in the clouds, the canopy of trees above. See the vastness of the world. Look down and notice shadows, patterns, colors, and textures on the ground. Sit or lie down and absorb your surroundings.

The act of cleaning thus enables one to sense the pure and sacred essence of nature. Nature's atmospheric changes teach us about cycles, change, and cleansing.

Trees and plants are involved in creating the air you breathe. Animals are breathing the same air. Other humans are breathing the same air. Focus on your breathing and look deeply into it; experience these connections fully.

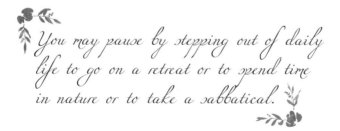

You may pause by stepping out of daily life to go on a retreat or to spend time in nature or to take a sabbatical.

Sit in a protected place alone outside at night or in a dark room. Watch your breath. Use your finger to point at yourself, and then point away in the opposite direction. Contemplate seeing yourself outside of your bodily form. See yourself in the trees, the water, the universe. Maintain a half-smile. Watch your breath for ten to twenty minutes.

Can you see how your choice of detergents, soaps, paper, and packaging affects the environment? Being aware of these choices is part of practicing right action.

Go jogging or walking and time your breath to your steps. How far can you go before you lose track of your breath?

A mindful approach to seeing is being in the present, without judgment, and taking a fresh look at the natural world. See the petals, feel their softness, inhale the scent. Experience the rose rather than simply labeling it.

242

Continually return to nature, especially to a familiar place where you have been practicing. Developing relationships in nature is not different from developing human relationships. Bring appreciation, love, and respect and you will enjoy a deep communion with that place and its ecosystem. Nature becomes the teacher of your true nature.

Get close, then really close, to something in nature you see every day but take for granted. Use a magnifying glass. You'll find beauty where you least expect it.

When you add extra awareness to your outdoor experience, your outing can benefit both your body and mind. Stop every now and again to really pay attention. This grounds you and deepens your connection to the natural world.

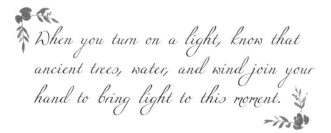

When you turn on a light, know that ancient trees, water, and wind join your hand to bring light to this moment.

In your mind, see a mountain lake with a smooth glass-like surface. A breeze sends ripples across the water. As the breeze subsides, the ripples do also and the water is smooth again. Remember this during the day, when something ruffles or disturbs you. Remember the image of the mountain lake. Feel the ripples and then let them settle.

Falling leaves remind you that nothing is permanent. When you watch the leaves falling and blowing away, feel joy. The changes of life are just as they should be.

Explore nature blindfolded with the help of a partner. The natural world will open up to you like never before.

You can shout at the wind to enter your house, you can pin a notice on a tree trunk, commanding the wind to come inside. Neither approach will work. But there is another, more effective way: simply leave your window open.

Going into nature, even for a short time each day, and being quiet will help reduce distraction in your life. Pay attention to everything you see and hear when you are in nature and you will be enjoying what it is like to live in the present moment. Nature gives you the opportunity to practice being in a spontaneous meditative state.

Meditate on the fabric of life in a natural setting, like a park. Think of the role of each living organism.

Air yoga poses relate to breathing for calming, energizing, or strengthening. Air poses include pranayama, deep breathing, and child's pose and they can easily be done outside on a deck, in a yard, or on the beach.

You have the capacity to embrace the waves of life as they move through you; even when the sea is stirred up by the winds of self-doubt, you can find your way home.

If you are walking for a meditation, simply be aware of the touch of each step. The feeling of the impact they have on the sidewalk, grass, or trail. Then stretch out your hand and touch an object, like a tree or flower, very gently and with great sensitivity. Understand the power of a touch. Rejoice in the awakening of your senses.

There is something magical about sitting in open space. Nature is a soft and grounding refuge. It can make you feel safe when you are struggling or feeling isolated.

Meditate on an acorn. Visualize it growing into a big oak tree. Imagine how the world will change around it.

Many parks have paths where visitors walk barefoot to stimulate health-enhancing acupressure points. Walk barefoot on a pebbled path if you have access to one, and sense yourself becoming grounded in and connected to each moment.

248

Picture a lemon in your mind's eye as clearly as possible. The lemon is as yellow as the sun and its thick skin is just a bit oily. Dig your fingernail into the peel and see the lemon oil come out. Pull some peel off to expose the white fibers of the pulp. Smell the tartness as you bite deep into the lemon and taste the sourness.

Learn to be aware of feelings without grasping or aversion and they can move through you like changing weather. You can be free to feel them and move on like the wind.

Here is a simple formula for creating good karma: Plant positive seeds. Have faith. Be good. Wait patiently.

Trees awaken with new buds in the spring and summer. They also bend during winds and storms. Trees do not think; they just do their work. Learn to become solid and stable like a tree, and be flexible, even in a storm.

Emotions like jealousy and rage become stronger when you bottle them up. Don't let them explode in dangerous circumstances. Go for a brisk walk, pound a cushion, or shout in a tunnel as a train passes overhead— just vent somewhere safe. Then see if you can work through the issues as calmly as possible.

Embrace all animals with your compassion. Wish for your compassion to ease their suffering. Protect life, practice generosity, behave responsibly, and consume mindfully.

Open a window and see how wondrous life is. Be attentive to each moment, your mind clear like a calm river.

Don't waste energy battling all the little waves, because the ocean is full of them and they keep coming. Let them come. Enjoy the movement and change. Just pay attention and correct the course when you need to.

Sun salutation is a yoga practice that you can perform in the morning, facing east toward the rising sun if possible. It is a series of yoga poses performed in a continuous flowing sequence and intended to improve the strength and flexibility of the muscles. You can learn it by watching an online video or attending a yoga class.

Boost your energy with a glass of freshly made juice. It is rich in vitamins, minerals, and enzymes, and maybe even contains amino acids, the building blocks of protein.

Meditate on the delicate veins of a leaf. A leaf's veins are similar to the various paths a life can take.

A plant-based diet is healthier, will make you feel better, and contributes to solving one of the biggest problems facing the planet: the fact that animals compete with humans for vital food. Explore alternative sources of protein.

Just before dawn, go outside and find a place to sit and watch the sun rise. As the sun emerges, be aware of the brightening hues of the sky. Is there pink or orange or purple? Rejoice in the beauty of a new day. Feel the rays of sun warm your face and refresh your spirit. If the weather is inclement, visualize the dawn instead.

Apes, crows, elephants, prairie dogs, and wolves all exhibit soothing behaviors such as grooming their stressed-out companions. Maybe we should emulate these creatures.

Breathe in and observe the impermanent nature of all. Breathe out and observe the impermanent nature of all.

The *prithvi mudra,* or earth gesture, is the joining of the index finger to the first joint of the thumb, but the palms are turned downward and touch the ground or rest on the knees. This gesture represents oneness with the earth.

Create a Zen painting. A Zen painting embodies the essence of an object. With black ink or paint, a brush, and some rice or bamboo paper, close your eyes and picture something like a cat or tree. What makes it such an object? When the image is clear in your mind, express it on paper with a few swift brushstrokes. Study the painting.

Acknowledge emotions for what they are and allow them to pass through you like wind passes through the leaves of a tree. Let them be without judging or getting caught up in them.

Check your inner mirror every time you look in a regular mirror and make sure you are a crystal-clear reflection of nature and its processes and take a moment to make sure your inner beauty really shines through.

Design a nature pilgrimage and use it to reconnect with nature as well as develop your inner vision.

The next time you feel the wind, try relaxing into the feel of it blowing over your skin. Surrender to the sensation without naming or judging it. Notice if there is a tingling or other feelings. Can you sense the flow of energy on your skin? Are you sensitive to the temperature? Try relaxing into the temperature and sensations.

Gradually shift to a diet of natural, healthy, simple, and appropriate food, away from highly processed foods, meat, and sugar. Give your body's chemistry time to adjust.

Take a scent walk. Visit a garden or forest where you can literally stop and smell the roses.

A rare person sees how far there is to go but remains unhurried, carefully placing each foot on the ground, delighting in the views and sounds but never getting lost. Such a journey is completed in every step.

To illuminate your mind, visualize a shining white letter *A* glowing like a luminous moon. Concentrate on that white light. Focus on it, then dissolve gradually into that light. Enter into the inner light and spontaneously awaken in the luminous dream light. Know everything is like a dream. Let it go as it goes and be as it is.

If you spend your time hoping that it will not rain on the weekend, you are wasting your time. Your thoughts do not change the weather. Your thoughts do not change anything.

We can all practice so that we can receive the violent words and actions aimed at us and transform them into flowers, like the Buddha. The powers of understanding and compassion give us the ability to do this.

Walk slowly upon crunchy snow or autumn leaves, attending to the crackle of each step.

Take a balance walk where you start out on fairly flat terrain and practice walking mindfully. Then move to terrain that forces you to maintain balance, expanding to the edges of trails or paths, embankments, fallen trees, rocks, and rocky streams. Notice your thoughts and feelings, too, as you work to keep your balance.

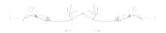

To talk a lot unnecessarily is like allowing thousands of weeds to grow in a garden. It would be better to have a flower.

Sharing gardening lore and swapping plants is just one way in which neighbors can benefit from a shared fence over which they can speak to each other. Value such occasions and make the most of them.

As you unwrap a picnic, rejoice in the outdoors and in the food that will nourish you.

A natural light energy meditation is a good way to avoid burnout and increase your level of Vitamin D. Facing the sun on a bright day, for fifteen minutes breathe in its inexhaustible energy through all the pores of your body. Feel the sun's energy convert into your energy. Feel your body become recharged by the sun's power.

Think of the path to enlightenment as an act of surrender, not an act of will. The river is already en route to the ocean. All you need do is submit to its inexorable current.

You have to learn the art of breathing in and out, stopping your activities, and calming your emotions. You have to learn to become solid and stable like an oak tree, not blown side to side by a storm.

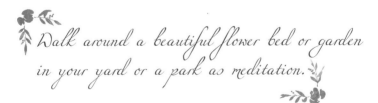

Walk around a beautiful flower bed or garden in your yard or a park as meditation.

Gazing into a calm body of water, concentrate on the reflections you see on the surface. Note how the surface acts like a mirror for its surroundings. When you go indoors, go to a mirror and acknowledge how you reflect your life circumstances and how you interact with the world. Is this what you actually wish to show the world?

If there is just one person who is calm in a boat caught in a storm, this person can inspire calm in others. This person can save the whole boat. That is the power of non-action.

During the summer, make a special effort to eat seasonal fruit for breakfast such as strawberries, raspberries, peaches, or apricots. Enjoy their succulence and fragrance, epitomizing the season.

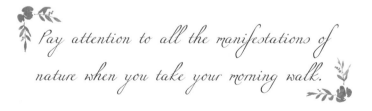

Pay attention to all the manifestations of nature when you take your morning walk.

As you rise from bed, be aware of your feet making contact with the floor. Be aware of the weight of your feet of the floor supporting your body, and the motion of your feet and legs as you begin to walk. As you take your first step of the day, your foot kisses the floor. With gratitude to the earth, walk in liberation.

A natural experience of mindful awareness sets in when you just lie down, look up at the sky, and watch the clouds. Experience the nature of how all things naturally come and go.

Sit next to a tree and make friends with it. Wait for responses to come to you.

Experience all things with the enthusiasm of a child, as if you were seeing them for the first time. Seeing requires no effort because your nature is seeing. Practice seeing each thing like it is new.

Trust the healing power of nature to flow into you during meditation or a relaxation practice. Don't worry about whether it is happening or not. Let your tensions flow out of you, down into the earth. Feel your body softening and opening. Enjoy the sensation of clean energy filling your being. Feel happiness.

When you use time wisely it is like stringing fresh flowers to the garland of your days. When you waste time, it is like pulling the flowers from a garland and throwing them away.

Consider how quickly you recover your balance if you trip. By the time you'd thought about how to arrest your fall, you'd be on the ground! Our bodies and their actions hold depths of nature's wisdom.

Meditate on the cycle of the sun as a visual metaphor for the human life span.

Imagine you are running through a dark forest. Then pause and take some deep breaths. When you do this, envision a clearing up ahead. You reach the clearing and rest there momentarily. Then you see a path leading out of the clearing into the forest and you follow this path until you emerge back into sunlight.

On the weekends, turn off your alarm clock and allow the sun's light and warmth to gently wake you. This will restore your body's circadian rhythms, maximizing your concentration.

With respect to the nature of the physical body, be aware of your posture, breath, and the interplay of the physical elements. Become sensitive to just how much food and sleep you actually need.

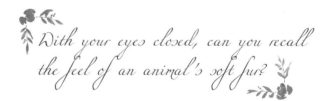

With your eyes closed, can you recall the feel of an animal's soft fur?

When you turn on the tap water, know that your body's essence pours out of it. Clouds, oceans, rivers, and deep wells all support your life. When you turn on the water, remember that water flows from high in the mountains and it runs deep in the earth. Miraculously, water comes to you and sustains all life.

There is a big difference between taking a walk in the woods and really being there in the present moment, and planning dinner while taking a walk or imagining the stories you will have about your walk.

The weather has its destructive aspect, but a harmless storm playing across the landscape is a reminder of elemental vitality. Watch the drama from a safe, dry place whenever you get the chance.

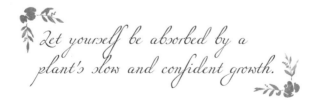

Let yourself be absorbed by a plant's slow and confident growth.

Look at the beauty of one flower. Stop and smell and smile. Breathe in one, two, three, four, five while inhaling, and one, two, three, four, five while exhaling. Focusing on the flower while breath-counting occupies the mind so that your mind doesn't occupy you. Stay with the flower for as long as you can.

Being free of false identifications is like going to a huge park and standing in the middle of a wide-open field: clear air, unobstructed views and movement, and infinite potential.

Meditating outside helps you to understand that you cannot control your environment. Letting go of wanting to control is a tool that helps you stay in the present moment, no matter where you are.

Pay attention to the aroma, color, and feel of a flower.

If you set up an altar, you can make offerings on a daily basis or every time you use the room or space for meditation. It is not just a physical offering, but also an inner mental offering. Appropriate offerings would be a small bowl of water and a few flowers, lighting a candle, or burning some incense.

Imagine that all your actions are like drops of water falling into a pond, and the ripples are signals you send out to those around you. This will help you see that all your actions have consequences.

Not harming people or animals you do not like or feel indifferent toward is a form of love and compassion that respects the wishes of others who are trying to find happiness and avoid suffering.

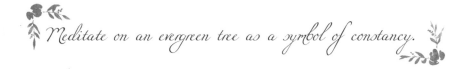

Meditate on an evergreen tree as a symbol of constancy.

Lie down where you can have an open view of the sky. Imagine that your mind is merging with the sky. Your thoughts come and go, like clouds through the sky. When your mind follows a "cloud," let go and bring yourself back to viewing the sky. You can also close your eyes and pay attention to your breath.

You are breathing all the time. Animals, plants, humans; we all breathe together. The atmosphere sustains you. You sustain the atmosphere by doing what you can to keep the air clean.

A lot of animals walk only a few steps before stopping to survey the scene around them. Take a walk where you take a few steps at a time. You will raise your awareness and find many treasures.

Organize a nature or labyrinth walk with a group.

Any time dark or negative thoughts enter your mind, point a bright light to chase them away, like the sun chases the rain clouds away. Make your mind a sanctuary for sunny, positive thoughts.

Connect to the experience of winter with a walking meditation, in the snow if possible. The path is beneath your feet. Make conscious steps on it. Count your steps. Walking along the path to enlightenment, connect with yourself by just doing what you are doing, one hundred percent. One step at a time.

Create a map of the outdoors around your home or the natural area where you most often walk. This is one of the best ways to become more aware of the landscape and its subtle features.

You can walk meditatively in water.

The butterfly effect is the theory of universal connectedness on a molecular level. A butterfly flapping its wings in California has an effect on the weather patterns in the Persian Gulf.

In springtime, follow the custom of the Japanese and search out the buds and blossoms of flowering trees. In Japan, the brief, sublimely beautiful emergence of the cherry blossom represents the sweetness and transience of life itself. Respond with your own meditative celebration of new life.

The electromagnetic field around all objects and living things is called an aura. You can learn to see auras. Their colors can reveal a person's inner nature, intentions, and moods.

Tend to your plants meditatively.

After a meditation in nature, come back gently into your day. Walk mindfully for a few minutes and then reenter your day, trying to retain the quality of mind you attained in meditation.

Imagine you are looking for a rare bird in the rainforest. Crashing through the undergrowth, you make a great racket. Result: you scare the creature away! Charging headlong through life, without stopping for silent thought, is one way to ensure that the object of your quest will elude you.

If you plant wheat, wheat will grow. If you act in a wholesome way, you will be happy. If you act in an unwholesome way, you water the seeds of craving, anger, and violence in yourself.

Dance under the full moon.

Spend a little more time where things are growing, giving off fragrance, swaying in the wind, glistening in the sun. A little nature slows you down and shows you more of the big picture.

Dance like a tree.

ABOUT THE AUTHOR

Barbara Ann Kipfer wrote the bestseller *14,000 Things to Be Happy About*. She has written more than seventy other books and calendars, including *1,001 Ways to Slow Down, 1,001 Ways to Live Wild, Self-Meditation, Instant Karma,* and *8,789 Words of Wisdom*. A professional lexicographer, Kipfer holds PhDs in linguistics, archaeology, and Buddhist studies.